62 &

PREGNANT

IT'S NEVER TOO LATE TO GIVE
BIRTH TO YOUR DREAMS

GRESHA P. LEWIS

Unless otherwise indicated, all Scripture quotations are taken from the New International Version, The Message Bible and King James Version from BibleGateway.com

Cover Designed by Kingdom Daughter Web Design, Madison, AL. Graphics used from pngtree.com

Copy Editor Krista Alecia Haraway - Elastic Editing, Huntsville, AL.

62& Pregnant

ISBN 978-0-578-46584-5

Printed in the United States of America

Acknowledgements

First and foremost, I would like to give honor to the Lord and Savior of my life, Jesus Christ. It is through Him that I live, move, and have my being. He has blessed me with the strength to complete this book that has been in the making for over 15 years.

I would like to thank my family for their love, encouragement, and support when I wanted to give up: my husband David Nathaniel Lewis, Jr. (he likes me to use his full name), my two children Chanette and Josh, my sister Stacey Archer, my brother-in-law Steven Archer, and my nieces Christina Archer and Stephanie Cason.

I give thanks to God for my fathers in the Gospel who used the word of God to uplift my soul, and to push me when I wanted to quit. I give honor in remembrance of Apostle Smallwood E. Williams (who laid my spiritual foundation), Apostle Michael J. Rogers, and Elder Oscar L. Montgomery.

Thank you Overseer Shaemun Webster for speaking into my life when I was at a low point. Thank you to my Spiritual Mentor Pastor Darnell Leach.

Acknowledgements

I praise God for the dear sisters, friends, and Mothers of Zion who have been such a blessing in my life:

Sister Louvenia Jones	Dr. Sandra Proctor	Ismeralda Moyet
Mother Katie Davis	Mother Dorothy Freeman	Theresa Pamplin
1st Lady Anita Leach	Pastor Robin Stevens	Shirley McConico
Prophetess Tamika Brown	Dr. Paula Tucker-Hogan	Bonita McCrimmon
Mother Linda Readus	Mother Amelia Hatchett	Theresa Lawson
Ma Leila Bailey	Sis. Deborah Baccum	Tamilene Black
Kimberly Oden-Webster	Ashley Daniel	Darlene Williams
Ma Johnnie Cochran	Janelle Latney	Pastor Carolyn Lucas
Catherine Smith		

A special thanks to Regina Jackson, Dr. Sandra Proctor, Christina Archer, Eloise McNealey, and Adrianna Humphrey for taking the time out of their busy lives to read my manuscript. I know it was a lot to ask, but I appreciate your YES!

And lastly, I thank YOU, the reader, for your contribution in purchasing this book. I pray that it will serve as a blessing to you so that you may fulfill your divine purpose.

Table of Contents

Chapter 9: Labor, Delivery, & Life After Birth

References

Chapter 1: Spiritual Pregnancy

1.1 God Promise is Your Purpose

Do you ever feel that it is too late to fulfill the purpose God set for your life? Do you long to know what has God promised you? How long have you been waiting for them? Imagine there are no obstacles in your path. What would you do to accomplish your dreams? Would you travel, get a high school diploma, earn a college degree, start a ministry, start a business, write a book, be a recording artist, or anything in between? Many people believe they are too old to accomplish their dreams -- but you must never forget that time does not stop the purpose and promises of God. Eternity is in His hands. He controls the times and the seasons of our lives, and there is a time, and there is a season for everything.

Let me assure you that no matter your age, God has impregnated you with the Promised Seed of Purpose. That's right, you are pregnant! Congratulations! Every promise that God has made regarding your life has a purpose: "So shall my word be that goeth forth out of my mouth: it shall not return unto me void, but it shall accomplish that which I please, and it shall prosper in the thing whereto I sent it." (Isaiah 55:11).

God gave you gifts to fulfill your purpose -- as long as you breathe air into your body and you still have a reasonable portion of health and strength -- your dreams, desires, and divine purpose can come to fruition. Paul tells us in Ephesians 2:10 "For we are God's handiwork, created in Christ Jesus to do good works, which God prepared in advance for us to do." God created every person on purpose, for a purpose. But it is up to us to identify what our Seed of

Purpose is for our lives and allow God to help us to bring it to fruition.

The Bible tells us that every good and perfect gift comes from above, down from the Father of the heavenly lights, who does not change like shifting shadows (James 1:17). What He has promised concerning your life, He will bring it to pass. Numbers 23:19 tells us that "God is not a man, that he should lie; neither the son of man, that he should repent: hath he said, and shall he not do it? or hath he spoken, and shall he not make it good?

When we look at the story of Moses, it shows us that God had a purpose for his existence. He was to be used as the deliverer of the children of Israel out of Egypt. The devil tried to kill him, but God protected him even in the crocodile-infested waters of the Nile. God prepared him in the house of Pharaoh and then allowed him to have a wilderness experience to come face-to-face with God to get instructions on his purpose. However, Moses was 80 years old before he knew what God had purposed for his life.

Can you imagine, God telling you to start a ministry in Africa, Iraq, or to open a business at the age of 80 years old? How about going into a studio to record the songs that you wrote when you were 25, and now, you're 65? Well, God wants you to know that it is time to give birth to the Promised Seed of Purpose that you must give birth to for His glory! If you are 45, 55, 65, 75, 85+, get in position and fulfill the purpose that God has ordained for your life.

1.2 Your Purpose is Your Passion

One may ask, what is a promise? A promise is a declaration or assurance that one will do a particular thing or that a specific thing will happen (Merriam Webster Dictionary). While we did not know how to explain what a promise meant as children, we knew what it represented. We made our friends pinky-swear and promised that they would not tell on us if we did something bad. If we were bold, we asked our parents to make us promises to buy us toys or take us places. Promises had a special meaning to us as children, and even more so as adults.

Like Jeremiah, God our Father had made promises and plans for us before we were conceived in Jeremiah 1:5 and 29:11. These two very familiar passages of scripture let us know that God has a plan for our lives. We may not know all of what He has planned, but we can rest assured that when He created us, we were implanted with the Promised Seed of Purpose.

Weeks may pass before a woman knows that she's pregnant. But because she does not know doesn't negate that fact that she is. What God has spoken over your life will not be revealed until the set time. The Promised Seed of Purpose is God's Word spoken concerning your life before you were born. The seed may be hidden until the time of intimacy with God. It is during your intimate time with the lover of your soul that He will speak sweet words to your spirit and reveal the purpose of your life. Let Him help you understand the passion that is burning down in your soul that you just can't shake.

When God impregnates you with the Promised Seed of Purpose, the fruit of these seeds will be brought to fruition in its season. There is a time and there is a season for everything (Ecclesiastes 3:1-8). The Bible tells us that a righteous person is like a tree planted by the water that will bring forth its fruit in its season (Psalms 1:3). While God has impregnated us with promise, there is a set time for the Promised Seed of Purpose to be brought forth. The longer the wait, the greater the blessing! The greater the blessing, the more of God's glory is revealed.

We are all familiar with the story Sarah. God could have allowed her to give birth when she was young, but He chose to show His power in a greater way by allowing her and Abraham to be old before she conceived. Both she and Abraham were beyond the years of having children. But God ordained her to be pregnant at the grand old age of 89 before the foundations of the world. God decided this time for greater glory.

Abraham and Sarah wanted a child because, like most married couples, they wanted to be parents. It was even more important for Sarah because in those days it was a shame for a wife not to bear children for her husband.

She desired to bear a child, and her desire was that Promised Seed of Purpose, that God had placed in her soul and spirit. In this case, however, the Giver of Life chose to wait until she was past the childbearing age to allow her to become pregnant and give birth to the promise. The seed had been planted, nevertheless, but the promise was yet to come.

There may be something in your spirit that God placed there when you were a child, a teen, a young adult, a mature adult or even a senior citizen. He put in you the Promised Seed of Purpose for you to nurture it to maturity so that when it is birthed, it will bring glory to Him.

Our experiences and passions prepare us for our purpose. God wants to use our experiences (good and bad) for a greater good. However, we can abort our purpose if we allow bad experiences to cause us to become bitter rather than better. It is God's will to bring us through those unfortunate situations, so that we may take the lessons learned and share them with others--to show them that we are a living testimony of how God brought us through the same thing.

The Promised Seed of Purpose is the thing that you are passionate about. The Promised Seed of Purpose could also be the thing that drives you up the wall. The place where there is a need that requires fixing, and you're wishing someone would please fix it! Well, could it be that you are the one to fix the problem? Often, we go into denial or feel someone else will see the problem and get it done. The issue is such a burden in your spirit, you are the one who God has placed the Promised Seed of Purpose to give birth to the answer to that given problem.

Jeremiah 1:5 says it like this: "Before I formed thee in the womb, I knew thee, and before thou camest forth out of the womb, I sanctified thee, and I ordained thee a prophet unto the nations." God knew what day we were going to be born. God planted the Promised Seed of Purpose in our lives before we were ever conceived. God uses our life experiences to serve as the ovaries, whose function is to produce the eggs of hope of fulfilling our dreams and passions with the gifts that He has placed in us.

Solomon tells us in Proverbs 19:21 that, "Many are the plans in a person's heart, but it is the Lord's purpose that prevails." We have dreams and vision for our lives, but those dreams and visions God will use for His purpose if we submit them to Him. If we had no experiences or trials, we would have no reason for hope. But God uses our experiences to bring forth the will for us to hope for something better.

I hope that you will recognize the signs of pregnancy, the process of pregnancy, the complications of pregnancy, how to nurture the promise to maturity, and how to give birth to the Promised Seed of Purpose. If we do not give birth to the Promised Seed of Purpose, it will hinder the next move of God, not only in our lives but in generations to come. God has given us the Promised Seed of Purpose to be the answer to something or someone in the Kingdom of God. Your destiny is connected to someone else. So, carry it with joy, nurture it, allow it to develop and grow, and in due season it will be time to get into the birthing position to push! Come in with me as we explore why it is never too late to give birth to the Promised Seed of Purpose.

1.3 The Anatomy of Purpose

For many of us, we took biology in school. Many of us had to dissect a frog to learn about anatomy and its function. We discovered that each part of the frog's anatomy had a purpose. The same concept applies to the human body. It has been said that the human body has 100 trillion cells, 206 bones, 600 muscles, and 78 organs.[1] One of my favorite Chapters in the Bible is in I Corinthians 12. There the Apostle Paul tells us that just as the natural body has many parts, so it is with the Body of Christ. There are many parts in the Body of Christ, but they all function in different capacities. He lets us know that if everyone were an eye, the body would not have a sense of smell. Paul goes on to tell us that in 1 Corinthians 12:18 "But in fact, God has placed the parts in the body, every one of them, just as he wanted them to be. If they were all one part, where would the body be? As it is, there are many parts, but one body." David tells us in Psalms 139:13-14 "For you created my inmost being; you knit me together in my mother's womb. I praise you because I am fearfully and wonderfully made." The Father reminds us in Jeremiah 29:11 tells us that "For I know the plans I have for you, declares the Lord, plans to prosper you and not to harm you, plans to give you hope and a future."

Our physical anatomy was created by God, and with each part of the anatomy, there is a purpose. As it is in the natural, so it is in the spirit. God has taken the natural things that He has created to teach us spiritual lessons.

Through this journey, we will look at the miracle of natural

pregnancy and birth and show how it reflects a spiritual pregnancy of the Promised Seed of Purpose in our lives. God has created each of us and has placed in us a Promised Seed of Purpose to be used to show forth His glory in the Earth. He has plans for us; plans to prosper us and to give us hope and a future. This is a promise that He made concerning us before we were conceived. "He is not a man, that he should lie; neither the son of man, that he should repent: hath He said, and shall he not do it? or hath he spoken, and shall he not make it good?" (Numbers 23:19).

God has placed visions, dreams, and ambitions in all of us. The anatomy of our spirit is still viable. These visions, dreams, and aspirations are still there resting in your spirit. You have been pregnant for a long time, and now it is time to give birth. *In this book, we will use the parts of the anatomy of the human body during pregnancy to explain the Anatomy of Purpose. Below, I will summarize each element, but as you continue to read, more detail will be given of how each part operates in the natural and in the spiritual as you move forward in giving birth to the Promised Seed of Purpose that God has placed in your spirit to be used for His glory.*

The Anatomy of Purpose includes the following:

- In the natural, the uterus is the organ in a woman where the embryo/fetus gestate before birth. Better known as the womb.
- In the spiritual, the uterus is the spirit of man. That place in which God places His Promised Seed of Purpose to develop to bring to fruition.

- In the natural, the ovaries hold the eggs until it releases an egg each month for possible fertilization.
- In the spiritual the ovaries represent patience. It holds our hope in place until it is time to be released to connect with faith to bring to fruition the Promised Seed of Purpose.
- In the natural according to Clár McWeeney of CLUE "Sperm are among the smallest cells in the male body."[2] Sperm is created for the intent of fertilizing an egg during intercourse.
- In the spiritual the sperm represents faith.
- In the natural, Clár McWeeney of CLUE also states that "The egg is among the largest cells in the female body. Women are created with these eggs which are released each month during our menstrual cycle."
- In the spiritual the eggs represent hope. When hope and faith connects an embryo is produced.
- In the natural, the embryo is an unborn offspring in the process of development.
- In the spiritual, the embryo is the Promised Seed of Purpose that God has placed in our spirit.
- In the natural, according to Mayoclinic.org "The placenta is an organ that develops in your uterus during pregnancy. This structure provides oxygen and nutrients to your growing baby and removes waste products from your baby's blood."
- In the spiritual, the placenta represents the Holy Spirits which provides the spiritual nourishment and removes those things

from our lives that prevent us from birthing our Promised Seed of Purpose.

- In the natural, according to E-Medicine.medscape.com "The fallopian tube in the presence of sperm and fertilization, transports the fertilized egg to be planted into the uterus." [3]

- In the spiritual, the fallopian tube represents our experiences that equip us for God to utilize us to fulfill our purpose for His glory effectively.

- In the natural, according to Medlineplus.gov "The amniotic fluid is a clear, slightly yellowish liquid that surrounds the unborn baby (fetus) during pregnancy."[4]

- In the spiritual, the amniotic fluid represents the Spirit of God which protects the Promised Seed of Purpose in times of trouble.

The spiritual ovaries are holding the egg of hope until it is mature enough to be released and realized in our souls. Our soul encompasses our mind: "So shall the knowledge of wisdom be unto thy soul: when thou hast found it, then there shall be a reward, and thy expectation shall not be cut off" (Proverbs 24:14). It encompasses our will: "Now set your heart and your soul to seek the Lord your God" (I Chronicles 22:19), and the emotions: "As the deer panteth after the water brooks, so panteth my soul after thee, O God" (Psalms 42:1).

All three (mind, will, and emotions) of these functions must align with your hope for your purpose to be realized.

As you matriculate through 62 & Pregnant, it is my hope and prayer that it brings clarity to your purpose. I pray that each chapter and every word resonate with you and inspires you to give birth to that dream, vision, or ambition that you have always wanted to accomplish.

I hope you will come to know and appreciate the vision that God has placed in your uterus (spirit). He has set an embryo of purpose in your spirit to be nourished so that you will bring forth His purpose. He placed it there from the foundation of the world. There are a special anointing and assignment that God has for your life and for your life alone. It is an assignment that no one else can do but you. The vision has been placed in your uterus (spirit), so you must give birth to that promise. No one else can carry that embryo that God has placed in your spiritual womb. So, carry it with joy, nurture it, allow it to develop and grow, and in due season it will be time to get into the birthing position to push! Come in with me as we explore why it is never too late to give birth to the Promised Seed of Purpose.

Chapter 2: The Promised Seed of Purpose

2.1 The Promise

Let's walk through the promise. The promise is that word that God had spoken over your life before you were conceived. It is the vision God had concerning you before your parents ever met before the worlds were framed. Before an inventor ever creates anything, he had in mind what it would look like, what the function would be, what parts would be needed to function correctly, and they even predicted the probability of the invention malfunctioning. God has spoken over our lives, and He also placed in each of us a Promised Seed of Purpose. He created us with a purpose in mind.

The Promised Seed of Purpose is more than just a great idea, gift or talent that He has given us. It was not placed there by happenstance or by accident. But it was put there intentionally to fulfill the will of God in the earth. What God has purposed and spoken over our lives may not come as soon as He speaks it, but it will come to completion. In the Book of Genesis, we see at the grand age of 75, Abraham received a Promised Seed of Purpose from God. Yes, in the spiritual realm men can become pregnant too! At 75 God told Abraham that he will be a father of nations.

I can only imagine the expression on Abraham's face when God spoke those words to him. But the Word of God says that He took God at His word. I wonder how that conversation went between him and Sarah. Did he even explain anything to her? They were senior citizens who lived in Haran for years around family, and now Abraham is telling Sarah, "Babe, pack up everything, we are moving." Abraham did not question God, but he stepped out on God's Word.

For Abraham to take such a leap of faith, I must believe that he had experiences with God in the past to make him know that He is faithful to His word. I believe that God has planted seeds of promise in Abraham in the past that came to fruition.

However, this promise is on another level. How can that which is supposedly dead come to life to give life? Abraham and Sarah had come to the realization that they would never have children. After all, he was 75 and Sarah was 65, and having a baby at that age was unexpected and according to man, impossible. There were no vitro fertility doctors back then, and if there were, they would have surely tried to talk Abraham and Sarah out of having a baby. There are too many complications that could arise in having a baby at such an old age.

According to the British Broadcasting Corporation (BBC), "Women who have gone through menopause will not be able to get pregnant without help. They will need to use eggs from a donor—or a frozen stash of their own eggs—to be able to conceive. For women, fertility declines with age, and fairly rapid after the age of 35, although it will vary for the individual." [5] The Mayo Clinic states "…that babies born to older mothers have a higher risk of certain chromosome problems, such as Down syndrome. The risk of pregnancy loss is higher—by miscarriage and stillbirth increases as you get older, perhaps due to pre-existing medical conditions or fetal chromosomal abnormalities."[6]

In the natural these truths are probable. However, with God age is not a barrier to becoming pregnant and giving birth to what God has purposed for your life. Before you were conceived, God placed in each of us a Promised Seed of Purpose. Many (like myself) have denied and procrastinated on the vision and call of God in our lives. You may even feel that it is too late for you to do what God has placed in your heart and soul to do. But the story of Abraham and Sarah will let you know that it is never too late to birth that vision that God has given you to accomplish. Did I say never? Yes, NEVER!

While the Bible does not say that Sarah had gone through menopause at the age of 65, she was probably in the middle of menopause, and surely by the time she gave birth at the age of 90, menopause had come and gone.

The BCC says that she would have needed an egg donor or a frozen stash of their own eggs to get pregnant. But God was the first to use the frozen embryo transfer by taking Sarah's eggs and freezing them in time to be released in its season. That spoken Word was placed in the spirit of Abraham and Sarah. That spoken Word could not come from anyone else other than the God of all living things. The Promised Seed of Purpose had to be implanted into Sarah's womb by God Himself. That Seed had Purpose stamped on Isaac's life even before he was conceived!

According to medical science, Sarah was past the age of conception, the chances of Isaac being born with a birth defect was high. But Promised Seed of Purpose was protected by the amniotic fluid of God's spirit so nothing could harm or destroy the seed. Note, God told Abraham his purpose and not Sarah. I assume that somewhere along the line Abraham told Sarah what God had spoken because in Genesis 16 we see Sarah saying, "Since God has restrained me from bearing children, go into my maid and conceive a child."

NEWS FLASH! God does not need our help in fulfilling His promises to us—He requires our obedience. Regarding Abraham and Sarah, the promise did not come to pass overnight, in a week, or even in a month, but it took YEARS! 25 to be exact!

Often, God does not move when we want Him, but we must stand on His Word and move when He says to move and trust His Word and His timing. However, let's get real for a moment: we have gotten frustrated in the wait. But it is in our frustration that God will always send us a reminder of what He has spoken over our lives. We see the promise given to Abraham in Genesis Chapter 12, and he received several reminders in Genesis 13:15-16; 15:4; 17:1-10. It wasn't until Genesis 18 that Sarah overheard the Word of God from the angels of God that she would give birth to a son. Her response was that of laughter and denial when confronted by the angel. I believe that was a natural response. She was old and being told that she was going to have a baby. Thank God her laughter and lying did not abort the promise. Thus, letting us know that the promises God has for lives are not contingent on what others say or even believe. The Bible never said that Sarah believed God. The promise was given to Abraham—he believed, and God brought it to pass.

As we can see, through the fallopian tubes of his experience where the ovaries of patience lie, God gave Abraham the egg of hope, and his sperm of faith fertilized inside of the fallopian tubes of life and then into the uterus of His spirit. Romans 4:18-22 (NIV) says it best, "Against all hope, Abraham in hope believed and so became the father of many nations, just as it had been said to him, 'So shall your offspring be. Without weakening in his faith, he faced the fact that his body was as good as dead—since he was about a hundred years old—and that Sarah's womb was also dead. Yet he did not waver through unbelief regarding the promise of God but was strengthened in his faith and gave glory to God, being fully persuaded that God had power to do what he had promised. Therefore, it was credited to him as righteousness." The Promised Seed of Purpose was birthed!

2.2 Promise Realized - My Story

God is amazing in all of His ways. His ways are truly past finding out. I didn't know growing up and even into adulthood that I was pregnant with a Promised Seed of Purpose. Like many women in the natural, I was spiritually pregnant and didn't realize it. God had spoken promises over my life that I was not aware of. But as I matured in Him and came to know Him more intimately, I realized that EVERYTHING that I have gone through has prepared me to be able to minister effectively in areas I would not have been able to do so without these experiences.

At the time when I was born, nurses were told to prevent women from giving birth before a doctor was present. I was a product of this decision, and it could have cost me my life. As my mother prepared to give birth to me, the nurses crossed her legs to hold me in until the doctor got to the hospital. My father was a dark-skinned gentleman, but when he saw me, he told my grandmother that I was the darkness baby he had ever seen. I think my oxygen was being cut off because of the doctors' decision. But God, who is the resurrection and the life, would not let me die, because I was pregnant with the Promised Seed of Purpose.

As a child living in Savannah, GA, at the age of around 11-13, my uncle and my ex-brother-in-law often molested me. If I said that I was going to tell, they would slap me. For fear, I was quiet. I wanted to tell my father, but I was afraid that he would kill both of them and I would never see my father again (I was a daddy's girl). God kept me through all of this, and today I am still standing whole and healed from the past. I recently saw my ex-brother-in-law. I always wondered what I would do or say if I ever saw him again. It had been over 45 years since I had seen him. I can honestly say, that God has healed me from the pain of the past. When I saw him, I felt no ill-will, bitterness or anger toward him. I was surprised! God had healed me from the pain of the past! Now I can effectively minister and testify to the emotional healing power of God.

After the birth of my first daughter, I begin to hemorrhage. My husband was saved and a powerful man of God. I remember after bleeding all night, I got up to call my doctor. He told me to get back to the hospital. I was so weak I could barely call my husband who was still in bed. Just as I was about to hit the floor, he caught me. I could hear him praying, telling the devil to get his hands off of me. I wanted to reach up and say to him that it was alright, I was ready to go to be with the Lord. But God said as he did in His word, "And when I passed by thee and saw thee polluted in thine own blood, I said unto thee **LIVE**"

(Ezekiel 16:6). He wanted me to live because I was pregnant with the Promised Seed of Purpose and He needed me to give birth for His glory. Today, I live to declare the Word of God!

In 1988, God blessed my husband and me to get pregnant again. This time, to my surprise, I was pregnant with twins. However, as I entered month seven, I went into premature labor. I was in the hospital for a week. I begin to have constant labor pain, but the nurses would not check to make sure that I was not in active labor. But around 11:00pm they decided to check. However, it was too late. The meds did not stop the contractions. The next morning, I gave birth to the babies. They were both under 2 lbs. The hospital did not try to keep them alive. I gave birth to Dominique and Demetrius. It was rough for my husband, me, and my daughter.

At the age of 39, I was a widow with two children. God saw fit to take my wonderful husband of 14 years home to be with him. It was hard. We went through some really rough days. I remember going over a bridge in Hampton, Virginia thinking that if I go off the bridge, my children would be alright. Their needs would be met, and my sister and brother-in-law would be great parents to them. But then God spoke a word to me and said, "If you do that you will never see the promise that I made to you." The promise that He made was that He was going to restore the years that the locust hath eaten, the cankerworm, and the caterpillar, and the palmerworm had eaten (Joel 2:25).

Today, I stand with conviction and great confidence to say, that

God is FAITHFUL! He has done just what He said that He would do. He has restored. The Promised Seed of Purpose was planted. I had to go through this valley to know that God is Jehovah-Jireh. He was going to use my life and testimony as a witness of His glory in the earth. My pain had a purpose.

However, I must confess that as wonderful as God had been to me, I was not always faithful and obedient Him. But He NEVER gave up on me. He had spoken over my life and every promise He made, will come to pass.

He promised that He was going to restore, and God did just what He promised. In 2003, eight years after the death of my first husband, God decided to give me a new beginning. The number eight means a new beginning. I had just begun to be comfortable in my singleness, but God had something else in mind. I wasn't looking for a husband, but he was looking for me. I had a dear friend, Exxie, who told me that my husband was looking for me and he was looking hard for me. My response to her comment was "I'm right here, why can't he find me?"

One year later, I was introduced to my husband David Nathaniel Lewis, Jr. We had a long-distance relationship. One evening as he was going back to the DC area, he began crying. I asked him, "Why are you crying?" He said, "I've been looking for you, and I've been looking hard for you." I told him to repeat what he just said, and he did. Remember, my friend Exxie told me that my husband was looking for me and he was looking hard for me. I had never told Dave about Exxie. I had been praying and asking God to make it plain if David was the man that he had for me and my children. I don't think you could get any plainer than this situation. I stand here to tell you that he is definitely the one! God has a sense of humor too. My first husband's first name was Louis; Dave's last name is Lewis. My first husband passed on May 23; Dave's birthday is May 23. What do you think? God is awesome, isn't He?

I always wanted to go to college, but I was never encouraged to do so by teachers, counselors or family. I was told to get a good government job, which I did. However, that situation of being placed under a boss that made me feel inferior and caused me frustration and pain was a good thing. His treatment of me provoked me to prove him wrong. He once asked me if I was "capable" of learning something. I was furious at that question. But the pain of that situation pushed me to register to attend college. At the age of 54, I received my Bachelor of Science Degree from Regent University in 2010. I am proof that you are never too old to fulfill a dream.

Out of all my experiences, I have really come to know who God is in my life. He has taken each of these experiences and used them for me to be able to share of His goodness and to let others know who He is and what He can be to them in their time of need. I Peter 5:10 is a reality in my life. It says, "And the God of all grace, who called you to his eternal glory in Christ, after you have suffered a little while, will himself restore you and make you strong, firm and steadfast."

Even at the age of 63, God is still teaching and showing me my purpose. I am still pregnant with the Promised Seed of Purpose. I know that I have been pregnant with His Word to share with the world.

I am pregnant with the spirit of hospitality. I am pregnant with an entrepreneurial spirit. I am pregnant with a spirit of leadership and training. I'm 63, and God is still revealing other Promised Seeds of Purpose in my life.

My answer to His call is YES! I don't always understand His ways, but I trust Him. I hope that my story will bless you and propel you into fulfilling your purpose—no matter your age or circumstances.

God, the Giver of all good and perfect things, the God in whom we move, live and have our being, the God who created all things by His word, has spoken purpose into you. Just because you have not realized your Promised Seed of Purpose yet, does not mean you do not possess it and you will never find it. Just because you have gone through trials that you never thought you would see the end of, does not mean it is too late for you.

At first, it may seem like there are too many obstacles preventing you from conceiving your Promised Seed of Purpose, or that it is simply impossible. But God requires closeness to reveal His Purpose for you. And to achieve this, you must start by developing your intimate relationship with God.

Chapter 3: Intimacy With God

3.1 From Courtship to Covenant

Intimacy between a couple should start with courtship. A man and a woman come together to get to know each other over a period of time. There is a courtship that takes place, then they fall in love, and eventually get married. They come into covenant with each other; therefore, it is such a blessing when a married couple comes together in agreement to conceive and bring life into the world. Out of their love comes an intense, passionate encounter with one another. However, intimacy between the couple was a process.

Let's begin your story. Jesus saw you from afar. It was love at first sight for Him. He approaches you. You found Him to be very interesting. You began to have long conversations with each other. You found that the more you got to know Him, the more you loved Him. You found Him to be very loving, caring, trustworthy, compassionate, and thoughtful. This Jesus was everything that you ever desired but did not think existed. But you decided to give your life to Him, and the courtship grew into a covenant relationship.

Now not only is He in love with you, but you are in love with Him. He wants you to be His bride. He wants to take you into a deeper relationship and tell you the secrets of His heart and purpose for your life in Him. You are now His bride—adorned for your husband. He calls you away so that He can reveal more of Himself to you. The Words of Love from the Lover of your soul say: "My beloved spoke and said to me, arise, my love, my fair one, and come away" (Sol 2:10).

How much more does He want to reveal? How intimate does He want to become? Well, not only are you His bride, but He wants to reveal secrets regarding your relationship that you have not heard or seen before. He desires to give you something that is just for you. He wants to reveal to you The Promised Seed of Purpose. What promise, you ask? It is a promise God has prepared just for you. The closer you are to Him, the more He will reveal Himself to you! You must allow yourself to become intimate with Him.

3.2 Becoming Intimate with God

Intimacy is a close, familiar and affectionate personal relationship—a close association with or deep understanding of a place or subject. To be intimate is to make known. It has been so adequately stated that "intimacy is not just physical, it is the deep bond of knowing."[7] This is what God is calling for. He desires an intimate relationship with the person He is to impregnate with the promise. He wants us to have a deep bond of knowing Him.

The only way to become intimate with anyone is to get close to them and get to know them. The time spent in prayer and meditation on God's Word will bring us into an intimate relationship with the Father. For the more we know about His word, the more we know about Him. The word of God says, "In the beginning was the Word" (John 1.1). "And the Word became flesh and dwelt among us" (John 1:14). We must allow the Word of God to be alive in us. It must become Rhema. David said, "Thy Word have I hid in my heart, that I might not sin against thee" (Psalms 119:11). He said, thy law will I meditate on both day and night. You do not have to read the Word of God every hour on the hour.

But we should set time aside to read and meditate on His word daily.

In his book "Promise of the Third Day – Your Day of Destiny Has Arrived," Bruce Allen writes: "Preparation for the Third Day requires stewardship of that passion and perseverance in the pursuit of the hidden secrets of the Lord. Consecration and separation are our commands. God's response is His manifest presence."[8] God desires to be close to us. He longs for it. In Exodus 19:11 it states, "Let them be ready for the third day, for on the third day the Lord will come down upon Mt. Sinai in the sight of the people," He wants to be close, so much so that He will come down to you.

In human relationships, the meaning and level of intimacy vary within and between relationships. Developing an intimate relationship typically takes months, even years and requires well-developed emotional and interpersonal awareness. God created mankind for intimacy with Him. Even after the fall of Adam and Eve, he longed for the intimacy of mankind. He gave His life to bring humanity back to a place of intimate communion with Himself in the garden of our lives (John 3:16). From the midst of the Garden, the Lord called out to Adam. Today He is calling out our names, waiting to share His heart with us, waiting to hear our hearts expressed to Him. This type of intimacy requires closeness. God cannot reveal Himself to you and impart His Promise to you from a distance. For the egg and the sperm to meet, you have to become intimate. The Bible states, that "faith comes by hearing, and hearing by the Word of God" (Romans 10:17).

3.3 Prayer is a Mindset

I once believed that if you didn't pray on your knees, you were not praying. I felt bad because I am not long-winded in prayer. The Bible tells us that men ought always to pray and not faint. Well, how do we accomplish that? We can't be on our knees 24-7. No, but we can be in a prayerful attitude at all times. We should have a spirit of prayer. As we stay prayerful, read and meditate on God's Word, we will come to know Him in a very real way. He will reveal Himself to us and unlock the secrets of the kingdom unto us.

Prayer is not always talking but listening. Intimacy requires a conversation between two people. It's not a good relationship when only one person does all the talking, and the other person can't share their feelings on an issue. Intimacy with God is the sharing of hearts. The Word of Gods says "Eyes hath not seen, neither ears heard, neither has it entered into the heart of man, the things God has prepared for them who love Him. But He has revealed it to those who are intimate with Him by His Spirit that lives on the inside of us. For the Spirit searches all things, yea the deep things of God" (I Corin. 2:9). That Spirit that resides in us searches out the deep things of God. We, in our finite minds, could not comprehend or understand the things of God unless it is revealed to us by His Spirit.

The Holy Spirit is intimate with God. He is one with God. God has given us His Spirit so that we can know the secrets of the kingdom. I Corinthians 2:12 says "Now we have not received the spirit of the world, but the spirit which is of God; that we might know the things that are freely given to us by His Spirit." The Lord has blessings and truths He wants to reveal to us. Many of us are holding on to hope and waiting for the spirit to reveal it to us. The more intimate we get with God, the more uninhibited we get with Him, the more we trust Him, the more we will get to know Him—He will reveal His secrets to us. Just as we seek love and intimacy in life, God is longing for the same with those that are His. He is waiting for us to spend private time with Him so that He can share with us His heart.

Psalm 25:14 says, "The secret of the Lord is with them that fear Him, and he shall show them His covenant." When we become intimate with Him, we find ourselves naked before Him. Our sins are uncovered. But He loves us in spite of our sins and faults. He loves us so much that He washes us in His cleansing blood and robes us with His righteousness and calls us His own. He does not pull away from us in shame but embraces us in love. He said, "If I would confess my sins, He is faithful and just to forgive me of my sins and cleanse me from all unrighteousness" (I John 1:9). What manner of love the Father has for us! You see, God loves to be close. He loves to cuddle.

As I was writing this, I was thinking, "God you made us, you know everything there is to know about us. There is nothing hidden from you, yet what else do you want to know about me?" The Lord said, "yes, I know you, but you don't know yourself. I want you to get to know who you are, as well as get to know who I am, then we can relate to each other on a deeper level."

You will come to know your abilities so that when I ask you to do something for the kingdom, it will not be a struggle because without doubt, you will know that the Great I Am is in you! "Ye are of

God, little children, and have overcome them: because greater is he that is in you, than he that is in the world" (I John 4:4). This will not only be scripture that you quote but a living word that comes alive in your life.

3.4 Alone Time With God

Intimacy requires privacy. There are times in a married relationship that the husband and wife need the children to go away to the godparents, grandparents, or trusted friend so that they can spend special time together. They need the freedom to share intimate affection with each other without the chance of interruption. God desires the same. He wants and needs that special time.

On a personal note, I once had a special place that I would go every evening near the water and spend time talking with God and journaling. It was such an intimate time with God. I could hear Him speaking so clearly, and I would write what He was saying to me. I did it so often that my husband asked if he could go with me. Everything in me (I would call it a Holy Ghost nudge) said to decline the request sweetly. But I didn't want to hurt my husband's feelings, so I told him that I was going to need quiet time—no talking and that we would be there for a while. He, of course, was agreeable. Well, after sitting for about 15 minutes, he got restless. I was so frustrated that it broke my concentration. I packed up and took him back home!

This was the time I was supposed to devote to the lover of my soul, but I decided to allow another, even one whom I love dearly, come into my intimate setting with God. The Lord later spoke to me and told me that He never told me to take Lot on the journey with me.

When the Lover of Your Soul tells you to come away with him, it is essential that we do not let a third party's feelings or wishes come in between our time with God—no matter who it is or how much you love them. A threesome is not a good plan.

I know there are those who have very hectic and busy lives, juggling jobs, children, and other daily activities. But I encourage you to take ten minutes of quiet time out of your day for God, whether it be before you start your day or when it ends right before bed. It might help to get a daily devotional journal. For ten minutes, pray, read, meditate, and journal about your experience. It doesn't take God all day to speak – but He does need your attention.

From time to time, God calls me away to be intimate with Him without the chance of interruption. He will say as He did in Solomon 4:8, "Come with me my beloved from Lebanon that goodly mountain and let me take you from the top of Amana, Shenir, and Hermon. Hermon is a mountain where the dew is pleasant, and there is joy there. Yet I want to take you beyond what is on these mountains." During the time I set aside just for God, He spoke to my heart and said, "For though the mountains you chose are good, I want to set you in heavenly places in Christ Jesus. I want to reveal myself to you. I want you to enter my presence, uninhibited, and without reservations. I love you, and I want to reveal to you my secrets."

Not only does He want to spend time with me, but I too want to spend time with Him. I want to reveal myself to Him. However, to share my innermost self to the Lord, to become truly intimate with Him, I must trust Him. I must realize that He is a true friend. He is someone in whom I can depend and share my secret thoughts. I know that He will not betray my trust. Intimacy demands trust. If you cannot trust someone, you cannot be totally intimate with them. I desire to always be with Him. For when I cannot feel or sense His presence, I long for Him even the more. My soul hunger and thirst for His presence. David said in Psalm 42:1-2, "As the deer panteth after the water brooks, so panteth my soul after thee O God. My soul thirsted for God, for the living God: when shall I come and appear before God."

In Exodus 33, we see Moses in his intimate time with God. Moses served as the mediator between the children of Israel and God. God declared that the children of Israel were a stiff-necked people. God in His mercy still wanted to have a relationship with His people. He called Moses into his presence to share the secrets of His heart. For you see, Moses didn't just want to know the acts of God, but he wanted to know the ways of God. It wasn't enough to see the Red Sea part or locust devouring the land of Egypt, he wanted to know how and why God moved the way He did (Psalms 103:7).

When Moses went into the tabernacle to meet face to face with God, Moses and God began their intimacy. God started sharing with Moses His heart and Moses his heart with God. He began to make things clear for Moses. Not only did Moses want to know God's ways but he wanted to see His glory!

3.5 From Desire to Revelation

The more we see of God, the more we want to know. It is true, a little bit of Jesus goes a long way. But I have learned the more He reveals of Himself, the more I want to know. I desire more than a little bit of Jesus, I want to know more! I want all of Him. God knows how to display Himself to us. He knows that we cannot handle all of His glory now. So, he reveals Himself a little at a time. God grants enough of Himself at a given time to satisfy our desire. Moses asked to see His glory, God said, "I will show my goodness." For you see, God's goodness is His glory! He wants us to know Him by His glory (goodness) rather than His majesty!

We should desire to know God's ways—his purpose, his heart, his holy principles, and even His sufferings. Why suffering? For in suffering we get to know God. In Romans 8:18, Paul knows that there is a reward in suffering for God. He says, "For I reckon, that the sufferings of this present time are not worthy to be compared with the glory (God's goodness) which shall be revealed in us." I have heard that many theologians and bible scholars preach and teach that this is dealing with the blessing of heaven, the glory to be revealed after we die and that we realize that suffering down here is nothing, compared to what we will receive once we get to heaven. Yes, that's true. But God revealed to me that once we have gone through a test that was meant to take us out, we will see His glory (goodness). "I had fainted, unless I had believed to see the goodness of the Lord in the land of the living" Psalm 27:13. We will look back and realize that the suffering was worth the blessing of His glory!

One of my favorite spiritual authors, J.O. Sanders, stated: "It would seem that admission to the inner circle of deepening intimacy with God is the outcome of deep desire. Only those who count such intimacy a prize worth sacrificing anything else for, are likely to attain it.

If other intimacies are more desirable to us, we will not gain entry to that circle. The place on Jesus' breast is still vacant and open to any who are willing to pay the price of deepening intimacy. We are now, and we will be in the future, only as intimate with God as we really choose to be." [9]

There are times early in a natural pregnancy that the baby cannot be seen right away. Likewise, in a spiritual pregnancy. You are pregnant with the promises of God, but the purpose of these promises has not been revealed. The purpose is only revealed during intimate times with God.

I recall a time when my pastor said that conception started in the mind of God. God told Jeremiah, "Before you were formed in your mother's womb, I knew thee" (Jeremiah 1:5). We must remember that God, from the foundations of the world, had you in mind. He already knew who and what you were to be. He knew your end from your beginning. God knew how many hairs were to be on your head; what color your eyes were to be; how tall you were to be; and who your parents were before they were even born. The promise was spoken over your life before you were conceived. He made promises over your life before your mother and father ever met. However, it is now time for those promises to come to fruition. He wants to reveal the Promised Seed of Purpose to you, so it is time to prepare to conceive that promise.

Chapter 4: Preparing to Conceive

4.1 Our Experiences Prepare Us for Spiritual Pregnancy

Like many little girls, I dreamed of my prince charming coming along and sweeping me off my feet. I dreamed of the perfect wedding and having beautiful children with the love of my life. And it happened! So, after about two years into my marriage, we begin making plans to get pregnant.

Preparing for pregnancy does not start once you get married and decide to have a baby. God created the woman's body for pregnancy even before she is born. We will discuss that later in the book. From the time of puberty until menopause a woman's pituitary gland sends a hormonal message to the ovaries to release a mature egg cell for it to be fertilized by a sperm cell. If the released egg is fertilized with the sperm, then the ovaries release the necessary hormones to the uterus that prepares the uterus to receive and nurture the egg. The egg then matriculates through the fallopian tube into the uterus.

In the spiritual, the fallopian tubes represent our experiences. Every experience we have is preparing us to fulfill the purpose God has for our lives.

In life, things will come that you cannot understand. For instance, you may experience being laid-off, losing a loved one suddenly, or your spouse may say, "I don't love you anymore." These things will cause pain and will cause your heart to bleed. This will have an effect on the egg (hope). But know that these changes are just preparing you to give birth to the Promised Seed of Purpose. While you are bleeding and cramping, your ovaries (patience) are holding on to the egg of hope, until it is ready to release that mature egg that will enlarge into your spirit.

God is taking all your experiences, the good and the bad, to prepare your uterus to be able to carry the promise He has for you. Roman 8:28 states, "For we know, that all things work together for the good of them who love the Lord, and to those who are called according to His purpose."

4.2 Nurture Your Health

It is imperative that our bodies are ready to conceive in the natural realm and in the spiritual realm. A physical is always a good idea before conceiving to rule out anything that can cause complications during pregnancy. In the spirit realm, we should assure that anything that can hinder us from delivering the promise—like bitterness, anger, or stress—is eradicated from our lives. We should examine ourselves daily to ensure we are walking in the faith of God. II Corinthians states, "Examine yourselves, whether you are in the faith; prove yourselves…" Our faith in God and the strength of His truth is what we need to ensure a healthy delivery.

Initially, a woman's body, mind, and soul must be prepared for pregnancy. According to Dr. Michael Silverstein, an obstetrician and assistant professor of obstetrics and gynecology at New York Medical Center in New York City, "There are things that can be done prior to conception that will ensure the health of the mother-to-be and also the baby. For example, it is important that women stop smoking before conception and to not smoke during pregnancy. About 20% of low-birth-weight births, 8% of pre-term deliveries and 5% of all delivery deaths are linked to smoking during pregnancy. Also, studies have revealed that smoking lowers a woman's fertility level by directly affecting the ovaries and decreasing estrogen levels."

In Romans 12:1, Paul admonishes us to "Present our bodies as a living sacrifice, holy and acceptable which is our reasonable service." Our bodies are temples in which the Spirit of God resides and should be treated as something special. We should not allow anything to invade our temple which will cause the embryo or fetus of Promise to be compromised. Romans 6:13 and 23 states, "Neither yield ye your members as instruments of unrighteousness unto sin, but yield yourselves unto God, as those that are alive from the dead, and your members as instruments of righteousness unto God…For the wages of sin is death…" Allowing sin to take over our lives will cause harm to the promise of God which lies within our spirit.

In his book "Promise of the Third Day," Bruce Allen states several things we must do to receive the promises of God. I believe these three are the most important in spiritual pregnancy: (1) "We should watch what we say because there will be a quick harvest of what we release;" or in other words, the power of life and death lies in the tongue. (2) "We must learn to love the God of the promise more than the promise of God;" so you must love the Giver more than the gift. (3) "We must allow the purification of our lives so that all flesh is burned away;" our will must be hidden in His will. Once we have accomplished these things, we are ready for conception.[10]

We cannot allow viruses that come from our experiences to abort the process of the sperm (faith) connecting with the egg of hope. We must avoid the virus! How do we accomplish this one might ask? I'm glad you asked. The answer is: Take your vitamins.

4.3 Take Your Prenatal Vitamins

Preparing our spirits to carry the promise to full-term will require a daily vitamin, which is God's Word. The more we learn about God and what He wants for us, the easier it becomes to discern God's direction in our life. This understanding only comes from time spent in His word. It will give us the necessary ingredients for a healthy delivery of the Promise. According to Dr. Carol Bates, assistant professor of medicine at Harvard Medical School and a primary care physician, "Taking folic acid prior to conception is one important way to ensure your body has a good supply right from the very start of pregnancy."[11]

4.4 Hope is the Key to Conception

Now that we better understand God's desires for intimacy let's consider what it entails. What does it mean? Is it hard to attain? Do not think it is not a challenging endeavor. It requires our relentless pursuit of an abiding and growing relationship with God. It is through our intimate relationship with God that the egg of hope meets up with the sperm of faith and produces an embryo of the Promised Seed of Purpose.

Your experience with God will allow you to know Him. That experience and knowledge of Him will produce the egg of hope. That egg of hope will be nourished by the love of God and will meet up with the sperm of faith that will cause you to bring forth that promise. The Spirit of God is like the amniotic fluid that protects the embryo from being traumatized during pregnancy.

It should be noted that an egg cannot meet up with sperm and produce an embryo without reaching maturation first. Hope is the anchor of the soul (Hebrew 6:19). Hope keeps our emotions from overriding our spirits. During pregnancy, hormones get out of control, situations arise in our lives and we often times let our emotions take over what the Spirit is saying and doing for our lives. The egg of hope grabs these emotions and holds them down so that the sperm of faith can find its way to the eggs of hope—so that the embryo of promise can be produced.

You see, even in a natural pregnancy when a woman's emotions are out of control, it is very difficult for her to become pregnant. Stress, doubt, fear, and anxiety can hinder the promise from being conceived. During the time of intimacy between the couple, many sperms are released only one will connect to the matured egg to start conception. The Lord has given many blessings. But there is a promise that He has placed in your spirit (uterus) that He wants to be nurtured and bring to full term. This is the Promised Seed of Purpose with which He has impregnated you.

Now that the egg is fertilized it must be placed in your spirit so that it can mature and incubate. The promise must grow to maturity. During this time of incubation, the woman's body goes through many changes—your spiritual pregnancy is no different.

Chapter 5:
The Complexities of Spiritual Pregnancy

5.1 Change is Uncomfortable

Pregnancy is different in every woman. All of my pregnancies came with challenges, and all of them were different. During pregnancy, the body goes through many changes. For instance, there can be slight bleeding in the first trimester—this is a good sign because it may mean that the fertilized embryo has implanted in the uterus. When the Promised Seed of Purpose has found its way into your spirit; there will be a sign that something is about to happen in your life. In addition to slight bleeding, you will experience breast tenderness, as this is one of the early signs of pregnancy. During this time, it is uncomfortable, but there is a purpose. The hormonal change in your body that is causing your breasts to be tender is really preparing the milk ducts to feed the baby.

This process excited me! The changes that are taking place in your body are causing a time of discomfort. The Promised Seed of Purpose placed in your spirit may find things that once caused no discomfort or things that did not bother you, are now an irritant. There are things done and said that now grieve your spirit. You must be careful and pray—because whatever you eat, your Promised Seed of Purpose is also partaking. Remember, the breast is a place of nourishment for your baby. When the seed is birthed you do not want the milk to be contaminated and unfit.

Another characteristic of pregnancy is constipation. What causes constipation during pregnancy you may ask? Well, the muscle that contracts to move the food through our intestines slows down, and if you are taking prenatal vitamins with iron, the results are an uncomfortable episode of constipation. During pregnancy, we must be careful of the types of food we are ingesting. Too much of anything can have an adverse effect on the body (i.e., too much salt). Drinking lots of water and eating lots of fiber is often prescribed by doctors for patients to avoid the discomfort of constipation.

As it is with pregnant women in the natural, so it is in the spirit. We must be cognizant of what we are feeding our Promised Seed of Purpose. We have something in our spirit that must be nurtured and protected from the time of conception until delivery. Therefore, it is imperative that we keep our spirits watered with the Word and eating the right food for the promise. John 6:35 says, "and Jesus said unto them, I am the bread of life: he that cometh to me shall never hunger; and he that believeth on me shall never thirst."

Also, one of the symptoms of pregnancy is fatigue. The body is working hard to support the fetus, but in the meantime, it is causing you to become more tired than usual. Likewise, when we have been impregnated with The Promise Seed of Purpose, we will often get weary in well doing. You may be like so many who do not know that they are pregnant with a Promised Seed of Purpose. You may be working somewhere and love what you are doing. But you know that there is something on the inside that you can feel moving in your spirit—you just can't identify what it is. You're tired and fatigued from working, and still unfulfilled. This something that is moving is the Promised Seed of Purpose that God has placed in your spirit. It is time for an intimate time with the Lover of your soul to ask Him about this movement in your spirit.

Another sign of pregnancy is frequent urination. The purpose of urination is to eliminate waste excreted by the kidneys. That's why water is so important. It helps to flush the kidneys and cause the body to eliminate the waste. When we drink the water of the Word, it will help us to eliminate those things in our lives that will hinder us from bringing forth the Promised Seed of Purpose.

The Bible tells us in John 10:10 that "The thief cometh not, but for to steal, and to kill, and to destroy: I am come that they might have life and that they might have it more abundantly." It is the plot of the devil to get rid of the Promised Seed of Purpose before it is birth because it will be a threat to his kingdom. So, we must drink the Water of Life to make sure that this seed springs forth healthy and ready to show forth God's glory in the earth.

One of the main signs of pregnancy is morning sickness or nausea. According to the American Pregnancy Association, morning sickness affects up to 85% of pregnant women.[11] I am so grateful that I never had the issue of morning sickness. But I understand that it can endure the entire first trimester. Morning sickness is the result of the hormonal changes in the body. While it is not something to worry about, it is an annoyance. If you can't keep any food down over a long period, you must see a doctor. When we are pregnant with the Promised Seed of Purpose, we will endure annoying situations. They may not be life-shattering, but they are annoyances, nevertheless. The solution for these annoyances is prayer. Our spiritual OB/GYN subscribes prayer to every situation. He tells us to "Cast our cares on Him because He cares for us" (I Peter 5:7).

He cares about every area of our lives—even those small annoyances.

Pregnancy is one of the few times in a woman's life when weight gain is considered a good thing. However, it is important not to overdo it. Weight gain should be gradual and under the direction of your doctor. For instance, if you are overweight when you conceived, the doctor may suggest that you not exceed an additional 100 calories a day in your first trimester.

Similarly, when you are pregnant with the Promised Seed of Purpose, you must be very careful about your weight. The Word of God tells us to "...lay aside every weight and the sin which doth so easily beset us and let us run with patience the race that is set before us." Being overweight in the spiritual realm can hinder us from bringing to fruition the vision that God has placed in our spirit. It can stop the flow of revelation God is trying to impart to us. Carrying the weight of a toxic relationship, holding on to bad habits, walking in disobedience to God, etc. is detrimental to you bringing your Promised Seed of Purpose to fruition.

Conversely, being underweight can also have an effect on the baby. In the first trimester, it is not uncommon for the mother to not be able to gain weight due to morning sickness. God has built in the pregnant woman's body protection for the fetus if the mother does not gain the recommended weight. Tiny fetuses have little nutritional needs, which means that your lack of weight gain early on won't have any effect on your baby. The Word of God tells us in Philippians 4:19, "But my God shall supply all your needs according to His riches in glory by Christ Jesus."

All of your needs to fulfill the promise that God has placed in your spirit will be provided by God through Christ Jesus.

Early in our spiritual pregnancy, we may not eat the right spiritual foods. We may also indulge in things that are not healthy to help our Promised Seed of Purpose mature. However, because it was placed in us by God, He will protect that which was committed for His purpose. "He is able to keep that which I have committed unto Him against that day" (2 Timothy 1:12). In other words, the Promised Seed of Purpose is secure because our divine OB/GYN is on the case!

When I was pregnant with my daughter Chanette at the age of 27, I went into premature labor in my seventh month. My doctor placed me in the hospital for five days. He took extra precaution and put me on bed rest at home, to protect my baby from premature birth. However, in my second pregnancy, I found out that I was pregnant with twins. Again, I had no morning sickness, and I went about my everyday activities. Yet again, I went into premature labor. Unfortunately, after being on bed rest in the hospital for a week, they were not able to stop the contractions. I later gave birth to two boys—Dominic and Demetrius. According to the Mayo Clinic, pregnancy risks are higher for mothers older than age 35.[12] But God had a purpose in mind. I was to have another child.

So, at the age of 35, I gave birth to a baby boy Joshua. Because of prior complications and having a history of premature labor, the doctor decided to perform a cervical cerclage, also known as a cervical stitch. This procedure is used when there is cervical incompetence and when the cervix starts to shorten and open too early during pregnancy, causing either a late miscarriage or preterm birth. During the pregnancy, I asked the doctor why I continue to have premature labor. He told me that sometimes there is a virus that enters the cervix that causes the uterus to contract, thus causing early labor. So, he decided to avoid this from happening again by performing a cerclage. It worked! I went full term and did not go into premature labor. On May 22, 1990, I gave birth to a healthy baby boy!

Just like the doctor took the necessary measures to keep me from going into premature labor; God will take the necessary measures to protect the Promised Seed of Purpose that He has implanted into your spirit.

Yes, there are times when women who have babies at the age of 35+ are at a higher risk of having medical issues. The baby may also have challenges. But with God, the Promised Seed of Purpose is at NO RISK. Age is not a factor in this pregnancy! Any nuisances or annoying issues are no factors in this pregnancy! Time and procrastination are not even factors in this pregnancy!

Even if your dream has died in your mind, He is the resurrection and the life. He can breathe life back into that seeming dead vision! You may say, "Lord, do you know that I am 50, 60, 70, 80+ years old." God will say to you, "I know exactly how old you are." Your reaction may be like that of Sarah, as she laughed at the idea of having a baby so late in life. But God's response to her is the same for you: "Is there anything too hard for Me?"

Chapter 6: The First Trimester

6.1 The Process of Pregnancy Begins

The miracle of giving birth brings with it many emotions. You are excited, you're anxious, you're even scared because you do not know what to expect. These emotions are exaggerated when you have decided to have a baby later in life—even more so if it is an unexpected pregnancy. But whether it is a planned or surprise pregnancy, it is a process. Even in nature, one cannot plant a seed of corn and expect it to be grown the next day. It takes time for the seed to germinate in the ground. Mark 4:26-28 says, "Then Jesus said, 'God's kingdom is like seed thrown on a field by a man who then goes to bed and forgets about it. The seed sprouts and grows—he has no idea how it happens. The earth does it all without his help: first a green stem of grass, then a bud, then the ripened grain. When the grain is fully formed, he reaps—harvest time!'"

There is a process that takes place in pregnancy in the natural and in the spirit. In a natural pregnancy, the term of a pregnancy is 40 weeks. What a process! No matter how excited we become, the duration of pregnancy is still 40 weeks. Throughout those nine months, many changes will take place in the body of the expectant mother and the fetus in the womb. We will explore the process of pregnancy in the natural and discuss how it relates to pregnancy in the spiritual realm.

6.2 Weeks 1-4: Unseen Growth

In **Weeks 1-3** of pregnancy, you may not realize that you are pregnant. While the OB/GYN has been trained in medicine and specializes in helping women with pregnancy, even they cannot pinpoint exactly when you conceived. They calculate the due date from the beginning of your last menstrual cycle, and in a way, according to their calculations, you are pregnant before you even conceived.

As it is in the natural, so it is in the spirit. You also were pregnant with the Promised Seed of Purpose before you conceived and even more powerful before you were conceived! God speaks to us through His Word in Jeremiah 1:5: "Before I formed you in the womb, I knew you, before you were born, I set you apart; I appointed you as a prophet to the nations." The Promised Seed of Purpose was planted in the spirit of Jeremiah before he was even conceived. Before you and I were conceived, God knew what He had assigned for us to accomplish for His kingdom.

But as it is in the early stages of our pregnancy, we do not realize that we are pregnant. Realize that, because we serve a multi-dimensional God, He does things in a multi-dimensional way. He does not place just one egg of hope in our spirit, but there are many eggs of hope that occupy the fluid-filled sacs (love filled sacs) called the follicles of patience. In the meantime, nothing happens until halfway to the time of your next cycle, at which time you ovulate. While there are many eggs in the follicles there is a set time for an egg to be released—this is ovulation. The egg is released and travels down the fallopian tube of our experiences where it awaits fertilization.

Once the egg is fertilized, it moves into the uterus of our spirit to produce the results that God ordained from the foundation of the world. When God plants a Promised Seed of Purpose in our spirit, more times than not, we know that something is different, but we are not quite sure what it is. We feel different, we see things differently, there's unrest in our spirit. Why? It is because the egg of hope has connected to the sperm of faith and produced a Promised Seed of Purpose. The Promised Seed of Purpose then matriculates through the ovaries of your experiences and is planted in the uterus (your spirit) to be nourished.

How many visions of purpose and ideas have come through the ovaries of our experiences? Our experiences (good and bad) have caused the seed that God had placed in us—before the foundations of the world to be planted in the uterus of our spirit—to grow and to come to fruition to bless to the Kingdom of God. As the embryo develops, you begin to feel different and even suspect that something is happening to your body.

God has implanted in each of us seeds of promise, and while the seed may be small right now, it is still there. It may not look like much, but there is no form to the Promised Seed of Purpose. You cannot see your vision of purpose—the ministry, the business, the invention, the gift of song—that God has put inside of your spirit, but as you continue to go through life, your experiences will cause that embryo to be realized as it grows into a fetus. At this stage in your pregnancy, you may not notice any outward changes. For instance, there may be no morning sickness, no change in appetite, no weight-gain, you haven't missed a period yet, etc. You may still have some struggles that you have been dealing with before pregnancy, but inwardly you know that something is changing.

I believe we were all created with hopes and dreams. Our life experiences have either pushed us to fulfill those hopes and dreams or hindered us from moving forward. Like me, many have discovered that we have been pregnant for a while and did not recognize it or pretended that this could not be happening. Some have concluded that it is too late to start working to make our dreams come true. But I have come to realize that with the Creator of time and space, it is NEVER too late to give birth. Ask Sarah, Hannah, and Elizabeth. Purpose and destiny have no age limit!

We were all created in the image and likeness of God. Our God is the creator of all things. John 1:3 states, "through Him, all things were made; without Him, nothing was made that has been made." We were created to be creative. Mentally, we have been created to reason and choose. This reflects God's intellect and freedom. Anytime someone writes a book, design clothes, paints a portrait, writes a song or poem, scores a film, names a child or pet, creates an invention, or makes any decision, he or she is exhibiting the fact that we are made in God's image.

By **Week Four**, it is time for your menstrual cycle, but it doesn't occur. God has a way of not allowing things that we are accustomed to happening in our lives to stop. He does this to protect us and to protect the Promised Seed of Purpose. You may not realize it, but the egg of hope is fertilized and is implanted in the lining of your spirit, so He allows the flow that sometimes causes the discomfort in our lives to cease, making us aware that there is a change taking place inside of us. It is when the flow stops that we realize that we are pregnant. There is a baby in our uterus that we must bring forth. God is setting your spirit-man up to be able to carry this Promised Seed of Purpose successfully.

There are things that He does that we have no control over to carry this seed. In the natural, after the embryo is implanted in the uterus, the amniotic sac is filled with fluid (the Spirit of God's love) to cushion the growing embryo, and the placenta (the Holy Spirit) is formed, which will bring oxygen and nutrients to nourish the baby. All of this is done internally. The seed is growing and developing even though you cannot see it.

However, it is our obligation to ensure that we eat the right food and take care of the outer man. We are to ensure that what is growing in us is adequately maintained. We are co-laborers with Christ in bringing this Promised Seed of Purpose to fruition. Once we realize that God has placed a Promised Seed of Purpose in our spirit, it is encumbered upon us to eat a proper diet, not ingest things into our spirit that could damage the seed or cause us to abort the promise. The enemy of our soul has come to kill, steal and destroy, but it is the will of God that we have life and have it more abundantly (John 10:10). The Promised Seed of Purpose is small, but it is attached to purpose, and it must be protected.

6.3 Weeks 5-8: Discomfort That Produces a Harvest

By **Week Five,** there are changes taking places with the embryo. It is still tiny, but its heart, brain, spinal cord, muscle, and bones are beginning to develop. The vital organs of the embryo are now forming starting in **Week Five**. The things that nourish and protect the Promised Seed of Purpose are consistently forming in our spirit. The continued growth of the placenta (that which provides the nourishment) and the amniotic sac (which protects the baby) is developed through the grace of God. This internal work is something only God can do. Paul tells us in Philippians 2:13, "For it is God which worketh in you both to will and to do of His good pleasure." In the natural, doctors cannot create a placenta or an amniotic sac (those things that help to sustain the life of the embryo)—only God can create them. It is in Christ that we live, move, and have our being (Acts 17:28).

It is around **Week Five** that you may suspect that you are pregnant. Not only are there changes in the embryo taking place, but there are changes taking place in your body as well. You may begin to feel nauseous; you may feel more tired than usual, and more sensitive in certain areas of your body. Things that you used to love eating, now make you nauseous.

Each pregnancy is different. For instance, with my first pregnancy, I could not stand the smell of fried foods (especially fish). I did not have morning sickness, but I just didn't like the smell of fried foods (not even my mother's fried chicken). I should have known something was up then, but I didn't realize I was pregnant.

In the spirit, when the Promised Seed of Purpose is being fed, there are some things that we just cannot tolerate anymore. We may not know why certain things grieve and weary our spirit, causing us discomfort, but it is because we are pregnant and further along in our pregnancy than we realize. This may be a good time to see an OB/GYN and start your prenatal care. It's time to go in prayer and ask God what is going on in your spirit.

If we are older and pregnant, our sensitivities are greater. We realize that we have waited to bring the seed to fruition, and we do not want to do or allow anything to hinder the successful delivery of the promise. So, what may not have bothered you early in life now causes more discomfort the older we get. While there is excitement and great anticipation of bringing the seed to fruition, this time also carries with it some discomfort. We must remember that in most cases, this stage doesn't last long.

By **Week Six,** the embryo continues to grow and change form. The eyes and limb buds are forming. At this time, with the help of the ultrasound, the doctor may be able to hear a heartbeat. It has been said that between two and a half to eight weeks that the baby is most susceptible to anything that can affect normal growth. It is vital that expecting-mothers be aware of anything that can cause harm to the embryo such as maternal size, weight, nutritional state, anemia, high environmental noise exposure, cigarette smoking, substance abuse, or uterine blood flow (even more so for mothers who are 35 and above).

Also, you may have begun to gain a few pounds, or because of the morning sickness you may have lost a few pounds, but this is normal.

Not only is there a change on the external but there is change on the internal. Your uterus which is carrying the seed is increasing in size. Note, the placenta is carrying spiritual nutrition to the Promised Seed of Purpose thus causing it to grow and the uterus of your spirit is growing as well. The external changes may be causing discomfort, but an environment is being cultivated to produce a harvest that we cannot comprehend. "Eyes have not seen neither ear heard the things that God has in stored for them that love Him" (I Corinthians 2:9). The Word of God tells us in 2 Corinthians 4:16 "But though our outward man perishes, yet the inward man is renewed day by day."

Even though God has graced us with His protection for the Promised Seed of Purpose, we must do what we can to protect the seed that is inside of our spirit. We cannot eat everything, and we cannot carry excess weight, such as bitterness, resentment, anger, and unforgiveness. We also cannot allow things in our spirit that will hinder the flow of God in our lives, thus causing spiritual anemia, we need to avoid high environmental noise exposure and spend quiet time with God to be able to hear from Him and Him alone. We cannot allow carcinogenic elements in our spirit that will cause us to get spiritual cancers which will eat at our soul and affect our Promised Seed of Purpose. Protect your Promised Seed of Purpose at all costs! You've waited too long and been through too much not to bring this pregnancy to term!

Week Eight is a big week of growth at this stage. Bones start to replace cartilage, the brain, spinal cord, and nerve tissue are now well-formed. The embryo is forming eyelids at this point. What is the purpose of eyelids? The primary purpose of eyelids is to protect the eye and keep it moist.

Conversely, the eyelids on the Promised Seed of Purpose represents protection from seeing those things that the enemy of our soul wants to use to distract us from the things that God has set before us in the spirit. The eyelids of the Promised Seed of Purpose will keep our eyes moist with the water of the Holy Spirit so that we can avoid any irritation, infections or cause blurred or permanently harm your vision. The risk of developing dry eye increases with advancing age.

Our spiritual eyes must be clear and healthy so that Ephesians 1:18 can come to reality: "Having the eyes of your hearts enlightened, that you may know what is the hope to which He has called you, what are the riches of His glorious inheritance in the saints…" Jesus told us is Matthew 6:22 that, "The eye is the lamp of the body. So, if your eye is healthy, your whole body will be full of light."

Also, not only are the eyelids formed, but the ears are formed. For us to hear the voice of God, we must have spiritual ears, and those ears must be attuned to the voice of God. He that has ears let him hear. For instance, when Elizabeth (the mother carrying John, a Promised Seed of Purpose) heard the voice of Mary (the mother of Jesus - who was also carrying the Promised Seed of Purpose), her baby leaped in her womb, and Elizabeth was filled with the Holy Spirit." When we have our spiritual ears attuned to the voice of God, it will cause our baby to leap in our spiritual uterus! No matter your age, your baby can still leap! Mary was 14 and pregnant and Elizabeth 87 when she became pregnant with John. Age means nothing in the mind of God, but timing and purpose mean everything.

Not only is the embryo changing and growing but continued changes are going on internally in your body. Your blood supply is synchronizing to go through the placenta to the baby through blood vessels in the umbilical cord. During this time, because of these changes, you may become moody. This is when we must be Spirit-led. Let's be real: we may be saved and love Jesus, but there are days that we are not so chipper. We have days when we are moody and really don't feel it or anybody, but when we are tested in this area, we must be Spirit-led and not self-consumed (as tempting as it may be). We need to get some fruit and make a fruit salad of longsuffering, peace, joy, patience, gentleness, kindness, and self-control (Galatians 5:22-23). Fruit is good for you when you're pregnant! Pregnancy brings about many emotions, but we must not allow our emotions to control our destiny. Stay focused as you move into your next week of pregnancy.

6.4 Weeks 9-10: Feeling the Promise Take Shape

In **Week Nine** your baby is still very small—about the size of a peanut. According to medical professionals, it is at this stage that the embryo becomes a fetus. During an ultrasound, you may even see the baby move, although it is still too small for you to feel it in your body. The same is true in the early stages of your spiritual pregnancy. The seed in which God has placed in your spirit has not grown to maturity. You may not feel it moving, but you have indications that something is happening in your spirit man, you can't identify what it is, but you know that it is something pulling on your spirit.

There are still no visible outside signs of pregnancy for others to see. Many times, you are growing and developing in the spirit, and you may not notice immediately. Others may not notice as well, but just because you may not see any signs from the outside, does not mean there isn't a difference on the inside of your spirit—it is this that lets you know that something is different. There's a passion on the inside of your spirit that you cannot quench, a fire that you cannot extinguish, a vision that you cannot stop seeing, and a call that you cannot deny. There are excitement and anticipation that is driving you to explore what is going on in your spirit. Your prayer life increases, you read, eat, and digest the Word of God on a most consistent basis in your search for answers. You take the time to spend intimate time with God, and there He reveals His secrets concerning the seed that He is given to you. You may feel as if it is not possible to carry this pregnancy to full term, but in the words of Bonnie Gray, "When you're pregnant with promise, don't turn back. God will carry your faith to completion."[13] You're closer to giving birth to the promise that you think.

By **Week Ten**, the embryo is still small, but it's looking a lot like a baby! The arms and legs are longer and can bend at the elbows and knees. The promise is beginning to take shape. God is now revealing to you more about what He has placed inside of your uterus (spirit). What was once the size of your fist is now the size of a grapefruit. Not only is the baby growing and changing form but your uterus (spirit) is also increasing. There's a larger capacity for your promise to grow.

However, while these changes taking place are exciting, some temporary issues may arise that are not wonderful but inevitable. You might put on some weight, you can't wear your size six clothes, or you may feel tired and moody—but fret not because these are just temporary inconveniences. You should try to think of these inconveniences more positively—you can now go shopping for new clothes. Most women take pleasure in shopping for new clothes.

Just as we have to deal with some of the challenges and inconveniences of pregnancy, the same is true when carrying a Promised Seed of Purpose for the Kingdom of God. Some changes must take place to make the pregnancy a little less challenging. We must change our thinking! We must realize that we cannot do what we once did before the pregnancy. We cannot wear the same mindset. The garments of our mind must change. Paul tells us in Philippians 2:5 "Let this mind be in you, which was also in Christ Jesus…" You're pregnant with a Promised Seed of Purpose, and that requires that our minds must change.

Romans 12:2 says "do not conform to the pattern of this world but be transformed by the renewing of your mind. Then you will be able to test and approve what God's will is—His good, pleasing and perfect will." It is the will of God that you bring the Promised Seed of

Purpose to full-term and to give birth to what is in your spirit, but we must do it God's way. Listen to your spiritual OB/GYN. He knows best.

6.5 Weeks 11-12: Stretch Marks: Your Badges of Honor

Throughout the pregnancy, there will be months when the fetus will have a growth spurt—**Week Eleven** is one of those times. Here in **Week Eleven**, not only are the fetus' arms and legs longer and can bend at the elbows and knees but now the doctor can hear a rapid "swooshing" sound of the heartbeat. There is a sign of life in the womb! Also, the fetus' genitals are developing, but at this stage, the sex of the fetus cannot be determined even by ultrasound. This growth spurt brings about new changes such as the sounds of life.

When we begin to grow spiritually, the Promised Seed of Purpose in our spirit begins to show signs of life. We start to see the outward and inward signs of growth. Outwardly, we begin to look different. What we use to wear with pride, we can no longer fit. In the words of an old Pentecostal song we use to sing during prayer service on Monday nights, "I pulled off my old filthy garments, and He gave me a robe of pure white. I'm feasting on manna from heaven, that is why I'm happy tonight." We have a new garment. We realize that God has placed the Promised Seed of Purpose in our spirit and we do not want to defile it or cause any harm to the seed. We may not be able to determine the gender (the purpose) of the fetus, but we know there is a purpose in the seed.

We are now, however, in **Week Twelve** of your pregnancy. The baby is viable, and this pregnancy is going very well. All parts of the fetus are developing even the tooth buds and toenails. At this point, the baby will continue to grow and get larger and stronger for the duration of the pregnancy.

Even those things that we think are not important to pregnancy must be carefully monitored. We must continue to maintain our inner and outer man to bring this pregnancy to term. Pregnancy hormones show their good and bad effects. You may notice that your hair and nails grow at a faster pace. There are even changes in your skin. It is imperative to visit a dentist during this time to maintain a healthy mouth. In our spiritual pregnancy, we must be very cognizant of what we allow to speak out of our mouth. The advice of your OB/GYN says in Proverbs 8:21, "death and life are in the power of the tongue…" Make sure that you speak life on your seed as you move into the end of your first trimester.

As we mentioned earlier, certain factors can cause a fetus miscarriage, like smoking, drugs, drinking, or a history of miscarriages. The chance of miscarriage is higher when the mother is older. According to the American College of Obstetrics and Gynecologists, "The number of miscarriages in the first trimester for women increases dramatically as a woman ages." [14]

Even though God has graced us with His protection for the Promised Seed of Purpose, we must do what we can to protect that seed that is inside of our spirit. You are at a place in your pregnancy where everything seems safe and secure, and you even feel more energetic, but you cannot take that security for granted and revert back to your pre-pregnancy mentality. You still must protect that Promised Seed of Purpose growing in your spirit. The OB/GYN tells us in His instructions that we are to "Be aware of the vices of the enemy, and that the thief comes only to steal and kill and destroy" (John 10:10). Just like he did with Moses and in the case of Jesus, he tried to destroy the Promised Seed of Purpose before the vision was realized.

You must continue to maintain a healthy lifestyle. While you may gain weight, maintain a healthy weight. Gaining too much weight too fast can cause problems for you and the baby. So, lay aside every weight and sin that can stop you from carrying the Promised Seed of Purpose full-term.

In addition to the other changes you are experiencing, you will begin to see stretch marks on your breasts, abdomen, hips, and buttocks. While they will not go away, they will fade after you give birth. Stretch marks are not cute, but they represent growth. The stretch marks are signs of letting you know that the baby is growing inside of the uterus and causing your stomach to grow. Many have purchased Cocoa Butter, Earth Mama Belly Butter, and Mommy Knows Best (just to name a few) creams to get rid of these unsightly marks on their skin. However, in the spirit, you want the stretch marks to show—it is an indication of growth.

The seed that God has planted in your spirit is growing. At the very beginning of your pregnancy, there were no outward signs that you were pregnant. But in just twelve short weeks, you can see the results of what God has placed in your spiritual womb. Paul talked about the marks that he bore in his body because of the Gospel in Galatians 6:17: "From now on, let no one cause me trouble, for I bear on my body the marks of Jesus." Unlike the Apostle Paul, I doubt if we will ever be physically beaten for the defense of the Gospel, but when we have a call on our lives to upbuild the Kingdom of God, we will be stretched in areas that may cause pain. Our flesh will be stretched! We must deny our flesh to become more like Christ. The stretch marks may not look pretty, but they are worth it. We should wear these stretch marks as badges of honor.

Unlike the various creams and oils that don't always remove the stretch marks like they promise when God stretches us, and there's pain—there's also a Balm that can heal the wounded spirit.

6.6 A Glimpse of What's Within

You are now seeing evidence on the outside of what is going on inside of your spirit. You are being stretched, and the baby is continually growing. By the end of the third month, the baby is fully formed with arms, hands, fingers, feet, and toes. Fingernails and toenails are beginning to develop, and the external ears are formed. Teeth are starting to form, and the reproductive organs are developed, but the baby's sex is still difficult to determine. In other words, yes, you are being stretched from the outside, and the seed is growing internally. But God has yet to reveal what the seed looks like or its purpose. If we know too much too soon, we may begin to allow carcinogenic elements in our spirit that will cause us to get spiritual cancers which will eat at our soul and affect our Promised Seed of Purpose. So, as you continue to visit

His office regularly, and have open communication with Him, He will reveal to you everything you need to know in the time in which you need to know it.

The Word of God tells us that "It is the glory of God to conceal things" (Proverbs 25:2). His wisdom and knowledge are unfathomably deep, His judgments are unsearchable, and His ways are past finding out (Romans 11:33). There are many reasons why God directs the course of our lives, and He prefers to carry out His purposes in ways that confound, surprise, and humble humans, angels, and demons. He's Sovereign! He wants to reveal His glory in us and through us. He is transforming our lives into the image of His Son. The path that He often takes us, we do not like it or understand—but it's for His glory. In an article by John Bloom, he states that "God doesn't always make His will clear because He values our being transformed more than our being informed."[15] As you continue to feed on His Word, stay in His presence, and receive your check-ups, your Promised Seed of Purpose will continue to grow. You will move closer to the revelation of the stirring that has been quickening in your spirit all of these months and years.

It is around week twelve in pregnancy that an ultrasound is given. An ultrasound is used to capture live images from the inside of your body. The ultrasound also known as a sonogram can help monitor normal fetal development and screen for any potential problems.

When I first got pregnant, I received a standard sonogram. It was in black and white, and you had to look very hard to distinguish the fetus on the image. However, with advances in medical science along with a standard ultrasound, there are several more advanced ultrasounds—including a 3-D ultrasound, a 4-D ultrasound, and a fetal echocardiography, which is an ultrasound that looks in detail at the fetus' heart.

God will give us a glimpse of the Promise, but with that glimpse, we cannot go off with a little revelation and develop a doctrine. Allow God to give you the full revelation of the Seed of Purpose. Don't get your Isaac mixed up with Ishmael. The glimpse that God gave you must be fully revealed so that you don't think what you saw was Isaac when it is really Ishmael.

I have seen many pastors trying to be pastors when God called them to be evangelists or called them to be teachers. Ephesians 4:11 says, "And he gave some, apostles; and some, prophets; and some, evangelists; and some, pastors and teachers…" The Bible also tells us in I Peter 2:10 that we should "give diligence to make your calling and election sure: for if ye do these things, ye shall never fall…" Remember this as you move into the second trimester (Weeks 13-28) of your pregnancy. You are getting excited and anxious about what is going on in your spirit. With 27 more weeks to go, you can't turn back now! The process continues.

Chapter 7:
The Second
Trimester

7.1 Carry the Promised Seed of Purpose with Joy

This is the end of your First trimester and the beginning of your Second trimester. Pregnancy in the natural and in the spiritual is a process—you don't get pregnant today and have the baby tomorrow. In a natural pregnancy, it is a nine-month long process. Your attitude during the wait will determine if it is a good and exciting time or one of dread and impatience. It has been said that life is a journey and along the journey, you will have good and bad days. You will have sunshine and rain—and both are necessary for growth. You will have peaks and valleys. The same can be said on the journey to the delivery of the Promised Seed of Purpose. You will experience life! Again, you will have good and bad days, peaks and valleys, sunshine and rain. There will be days when all you want to do is get through another day without any complications.

The second trimester of pregnancy is a time of some relief. You realize that many of the issues you had in your first trimester are now subsiding. The morning sickness, the fatigue, and the mood swings are fading, and you now have more energy. You are even more excited about what is going on in your spirit. In the spirit, you are getting adjusted to the new life growing inside the womb of your spirit. The unsettling you once experienced is now subsiding. The Lord, your OB/GYN, has spoken peace. He has promised to be with you every step of the way during this pregnancy and beyond. What you are carrying is for the benefit of His kingdom. He is going to protect you and the Promise in your spirit.

At the beginning of this pregnancy, you had no idea that you were pregnant. You had been going through life, not realizing that the dreams and ambitions that you had since childhood were the seeds that God placed in your spirit before you were ever conceived. Your Promised Seed of Purpose can be called the Jeremiah 29:11 Seed: "For I know the thoughts that I think toward you, says the Lord, thoughts of peace and not of evil, to give you a future and a hope." You may have given up on those dreams and ambitions and thought that it is too late to accomplish them. But you didn't realize that God can resurrect those dead dreams and aspirations. In your mind and in the minds of others, you may think you are too old to accomplish the goal. But ask Abraham, Sarah, Hannah, and Elizabeth and they will all tell you that it is never too late. You can still conceive and carry that Promised Seed of Purpose to full term.

We must realize that God is the Father of time. He is never late and never too early. He's an on-time God! As you know, His time and our time are two different things. Sunday Adelaja once said that "time has only one Lord-God."[16] Our times are in His hands. Trust His timing. Remain cognizant of the challenges that can cause you not to bring the Promised Seed of Purpose to fruition.

7.2 God Wants to Carry Your Weight

As time has passed, and you now realize that you are pregnant, this baby is causing many changes to your body. The pregnancy is progressing well, but there are still changes going on that are challenging. For instance, the extra weight that you are now carrying may cause you to have backaches.

In a natural pregnancy, weight gain is permitted, but not in the spiritual pregnancy. In a spiritual pregnancy, God wants to carry our weight. He tells us to "Cast all our cares on Him for He cares for us (1 Peter 5:7). He tells us to lay aside every weight and sin that so easily beset us" (Hebrews 12:1). The cares of this life are distractions that keep us from bringing forth the Promised Seed of Purpose. Too much weight in the natural is bad for you and the baby. You can get toxemia which is detrimental to you and the baby's well-being. In the spiritual, weight can have the same effect. It can cause you to abort the promise before it is brought to fruition.

In addition to weight gain, the changes in your hormones may cause your gums to bleed and your mouth to be sore. In the natural when these inconveniences in pregnancy take place, women sometimes complain and gripe about all the issues going on in their body. However, in the spiritual pregnancy, you must watch what you are speaking over yourself because it will affect the Promised Seed of Purpose growing in your spirit. The Lord (your OB/GYN) gives instructions regarding your mouth. He says that "Words satisfy the mind as much as fruit does the stomach and good talk is as gratifying as a good harvest. Words kill, words give life; they're either poison or fruit—you choose" (Proverbs 18:20-21 - MSG). So be careful of what comes out of your mouth during this pregnancy. You do not want to speak death over the Promised Seed of Purpose. You've waited too long to give birth not to carry to full-term.

Through this process of pregnancy, as in life, you will continue to have distractions. Make sure that distractions do not cause you to lose sight of the promise. In a natural pregnancy, you may continue to have the distractions of headaches, hair growth (in places you prefer not to grow) discharge, and breast enlargement with tenderness. Remember, that even some of these inconveniences have a purpose. For instance, if the discharge is green or yellow, this is an indication that there is an infection, and that a doctor needs to be called.

In the spiritual pregnancy, if the enemy has caused a situation in your life that can cause harm to you and your Promised Seed of Purpose, you can call your OB/GYN to have Him prescribe the Balm to cure the unwanted condition. He can speak a word to kill the bacteria that is causing the infection. Whatever foreign entity (i.e., fear, doubt, weariness, etc.) that tries to attach itself to your spirit, call your OB/GYN immediately. Because not only is He an OB/GYN but He is a specialist in all types of infections. In the natural and in the spiritual, many other inconveniences take place during pregnancy; remember that all of these are just temporary inconveniences. Your baby is growing quickly at this point, and its form is now more distinguishable. The baby's eyes are moving into position, the ankles and wrists have formed, and though the head is still disproportionately big, the rest of the body is starting to catch up. The process continues.

7.3 Week 13: The Waning Appetite and Passion

At **13 weeks**, you've grown a fetus that has vocal cords, teeth, and even fingerprints that only he/she has (wow!). Your baby has its own identity! Just like the baby's fingerprints gives him/her their own identity, God has given you a dream, a vision, and a purpose that no one else can fulfill but you. He chose you for that purpose, and He chose that purpose for His glory and in His timing. Your Promised Seed of Purpose has its own identity!

As you grow spiritually, the Promised Seed of Purpose will grow and be strengthened. Remember, as your Seed of Purpose grows your spirit will grow—you grow together. What is growing on the inside of your spirit is now showing on the outside. Others can see something is going on inside of your spirit. Their excitement will also cause you to be more excited and rejuvenated. The fatigue, uncertainty, and sickness that you experienced at the beginning of the pregnancy is subsiding, and now you are re-energized. Not only has your appetite returned but your passion has increased. Even when you know that you are pregnant with the Promised Seed of Purpose, there are days when your appetite and passion will wane. It requires us to push when we want to lie down. It requires us to read and embrace the Word of God when we want to just look at the book from a distance. (*Oh, maybe I'm the only one who goes through this! – lol!*) Being pregnant in the natural and in the spirit requires us to move past our feelings.

However, during this time, you will continue to gain weight, but remember as in **Week 12**, do not gain too much weight because it can cause complications. Be conscious of what and how much you eat. Make sure you are not eating from the table of every wind of doctrine that can cause harm for your Seed. You are the Carrier of the Seed (the adult in this situation). So, "be no longer children, tossed to and fro and carried about with every wind of doctrine by the sleight of men and their cunning and craftiness, whereby they lie in wait to deceive"

(Ephesians 4:14). What they serve may sound good--the ingredients may be things that you have heard in the Gospel, but once you start eating what they are serving there may be ingredients they have not disclosed that will harm the Promise. Be careful of what you eat!

7.4 Week 14: Change Your Clothes

Your baby is still growing and is about the size of a peach. If you have a sonogram at this point, you would see the baby wiggling his or her toes and may even be thumb sucking! You can now see the signs of life in the Promise.

Inconveniences will continue to reoccur in your life. Life goes on, pregnant or not. You may still experience aches and pains in your body in the natural as well as in your spirit. As you get closer to giving birth to what God has purposed for your life, you will experience things that you never saw coming. They are just distractions. In the natural, one of the issues that may arise may include ligament pains which are aches and pains as your muscles and ligaments stretched to accommodate your growing baby. A couple of the things that may happen during this time that you may want to continue even after the pregnancy, such as hair growth (just on your head), breast enlargement, and increased energy.

These signs are letting you know that you and your Promised Seed of Purpose are growing. There is life on the inside of your spirit! What you thought was dead is very much alive. So, because you are growing on the inside and the outside, you now must change your clothing. You cannot wear the same clothes you once wore. Those skinny jeans cannot go over your stomach. If you try, you will be uncomfortable.

Once we have been pregnant with the Promised Seed of Purpose, there are things that we must do to make sure that what we are carrying is not contaminated with something that will harm or abort it. When I speak of having to change our clothing, I am not talking of physical clothing, but spiritual. A woman wearing pants has nothing to do with the Seed of Purpose God placed inside her spirit.

Clothing on a spiritual level means to make sure that you are in right standing with God. Let us go back to the Garden of Eden. When Adam and Eve sinned, the first thing they did was to cover themselves with fig leaves because they were ashamed of what they had done. They were naked thus, not in right standing with God. To rectify that issue, God covered them with animal skin thus making atonement for their sin. Genesis 3:21 states that God "Made for Adam and for his wife garments of skins and clothed them." God had to sacrifice an animal to show them how to make atonement for sin. It was this atonement that caused them to regain the covenant relationship with God. Therefore, their clothing became constant reminders to us of the atonement that would be made on our behalf and our covenant with God.

It is encumbered upon us who are carrying the Promised Seed of Purpose to make sure that we are forever covered by the blood of Jesus and His righteousness. We must make sure that we come before God when we have sinned so that He can clothe us in His righteousness. We cannot harbor sin and think that it will not affect the Promised Seed of

Purpose--we must change our clothes. Take off things that do not fit the Purpose for our life. They may have once been comfortable but are now too tight. They may be outfits that you have always liked. But they will not look good on the Purpose. So, your wardrobe must change. It is too tight and doesn't fit! Take it off as we move into **Week 15**.

7.5 Week 15: Check-Ups That Shake Your Foundation

Great news! You and your baby are doing well! Everything is progressing as expected. There has been nothing out of the ordinary taking place. You're eating well providing the necessary nourishment for the baby to grow and for you to remain healthy. As you continue to feed on the Word of God, stay in a relationship with Him through prayer, the Promised Seed of Purpose and your spirit will continue to grow.

In the natural, as an older woman, the doctor may recommend or even insist on other tests to make sure that the baby is healthy and that there are no complications. These tests may include a blood test called the quadruple marker screening which tests for Down Syndrome; or an amniocentesis which tests a small sample of the amniotic fluid. While these tests in the natural can give information about what is going on with the baby, they can also cause anxiety with the mother (especially a woman who is older). According to Webmd.com "There is a small risk that an amniocentesis could cause a miscarriage (less than 1%, or approximately 1 in 200 to 1 in 400)." [17]

Trials only come to make us strong. This is true, but some tests will shake us to the core! Even though we are standing on the promises of God, some tests shake our foundation. Storms do not cease because Jesus is onboard neither will test stop because we are surrounded by the love of God. When trials come, they are often sent to distract and abort our purpose. Because we are surrounded by the love of God, He will never allow any test to abort the purpose that He is placed in our spirit for His glory. His glory cannot be aborted! James tells us, "Knowing this, that the trying of your faith worketh patience. But let patience have her perfect work, that ye may be perfect and entire, wanting nothing." (James 1:3-4)

We must be patient in the process. It is in the process that we often see the ways of God. Psalms 103:7 "He made known His ways to Moses, His acts to the children of Israel." To know God's ways is to know who He is and to know His acts is to know what He does. When we come to understand who He is, we will be able to go through the process of bringing the Promised Seed of Purpose to fruition. You will have the confidence to know that the One who calls you is faithful, and He will do it (1 Thessalonians 5:24). Because you understand His ways, you recognize the difference between the time you are anointed for something and the time God appoints for you to walk in it. For instance, David was anointed to be king as a boy but did not step into the position until he was around 30 years old. You are anointed and appointed for the assignment but wait on the timing of God. As you and the baby continue to grow, you may need extra support for your legs and back while you are walking and sleeping.

You need something or someone to lift you in prayer and encouragement during this time. Don't be afraid to ask for support. If your legs get weak along the way, exercise your faith and if your faith is weak, ask someone to support you. You are moving into a new phase of your pregnancy. You're about to get some exciting news—if you want to know.

7.6 Week 16: Watch Your Mouth

You have just entered **Week 16** of your pregnancy. Things are getting really exciting now. You may have another prenatal visit this week, where you will get to hear the baby's heartbeat again. Even more thrilling will be feeling the baby kick, which could happen to start this week, so pay attention to those subtle feelings in your pregnant belly.

I remember when I felt my daughter move for the first time. I was lying on the bed talking to one of the mothers from the church. We were laughing and having a good time. She was sharing stories with me about her own pregnancies. Suddenly, I felt this weird sensation in my stomach, and I screamed! I was flipping out because it wasn't something that I had experienced before. In a hilarious calm voice, she said, "Girl, that's your baby moving." I was too excited. I wanted to have that feeling all the time.

Another cool fact is that the baby is starting to be able to hear your voice—and he or she will recognize it at birth—so feel free to chat baby up any chance you get. It is imperative that what you speak are words of life and not words of death.

I knew a woman who got pregnant late in life. It was an unwanted pregnancy, and she spoke words of death over that fetus. She gave birth to a fetus with many abnormalities and one who could not live. The sad thing about this situation is that she realized the words of death that she spoke over her baby in her womb came to pass. The power of life and death is in the tongue. This scripture became a reality in her life.

In my fifth or sixth month of pregnancy, my first husband and I would talk to the babies while they were in the womb. When we would talk to them, they would move so much. It was hilarious and fun for both of us. It brought joy for us to see the evidence of what was going inside my womb displaying itself externally. Speaking life to the Promised Seed of Purpose will cause it to move in your spirit and bring joy as well. Speak over your promise, encourage your Promise.

7.7 Week 17: Purpose Delayed But Never Denied

Can you believe it? You are now in **Week 17** of your pregnancy. The fertilized egg is now about the size of a pomegranate. You are beginning to think about gender. What color should you paint the baby's room? What will you name the baby?

At this point, the doctor may be able to tell you the gender of the baby, if you want to know. As you draw closer to delivery, you will have a break from some of the annoyances of life. But remember tests and trials will continue from time to time. In the natural, there may be discharge, weird dreams, your breast and stomach may itch because it is stretching, more stretch marks may appear, and you may gain more weight. Again, they are just annoyances and distractions that are all a part of the process.

The baby's working on getting stronger, and as this happens, the rubbery cartilage is now turning to bone. The baby's growing some meat on those bones, putting on some fat. While your Promised Seed of Purpose gets stronger, God is sustaining your spirit.

Amid these distractions, God will share things that He wants you to do regarding His purpose. Some of the things that He reveals may not make sense to the natural mind. Go with it anyway. He may tell you to get a passport. He may say to you to go look at an office space—go with it. He may tell you to go look at a house—go with it, even if you have no money and your credit is less than perfect. There are times when you cannot see the promise, but someone God has revealed His purpose to regarding your life will speak a word to you. You may not see it, but God may use someone to nourish that seed in you.

While I was at Regent, I presented a paper in class about my non-profit organization. After class, my professor said to me that the program that I shared had a special anointing on it and that I would be going south (I can't remember all the states he mentioned, but I remembered Alabama). I remembered Alabama because my first husband (Louis, who passed away), and I had planned on moving to Alabama after he retired. After he died, I knew that that dream would never come to fruition. When the professor said that I thought, "I don't know how that will come to pass." My new husband (David) and I had just purchased a new house in Yorktown and moving was not in our plans.

Some months later, the government agency my husband David worked for told him that they were moving him to Alabama. He had to choose whether to stay in the VA area or go to Alabama—so we decided to go to Alabama. The dream that I thought had died with my first husband was resurrected—because it was purposed for me to come to Alabama before I was formed in my mother's womb. God is awesome!

This dream did not come to pass when I was in my 30's or 40's, but when I was 55! Louis and I were pregnant with the vision and dream of moving to Alabama around 1987, but it did not come to fruition until 2011.

In the Word of God, we see several instances where the Promised Seed of Purpose was delayed, but it was never denied. They were all delayed until it was time for God's glory to be revealed. We see Abraham and Sarah trying to help God in fulfilling what He had already purposed before they were even born. God chose to delay the Promise until they were too old so that He would get the glory! Isaac was the Promised Seed of Purpose, not Ishmael! Sarah was purposed to give birth to the Promised Seed - not Hagar.

Then we go to the New Testament and see Elizabeth being pregnant in her old age. Even though Zachariah's mouth got him in trouble and God had to cause him not to talk until the Promise was birthed, it was delayed for the glory of God. There may be times when God does not want to reveal your pregnancy so that you or no one else can speak negativity over the Seed of Purpose. Some people mean well, but they can be very discouraging, especially when you are trying to fulfill that dream or vision late in life.

So, you, like Elizabeth, you may have to keep your dreams and visions a secret for a while. The Bible says, "After this his wife Elizabeth became pregnant and for five months remained in seclusion. Until now you have been able to keep this incredible news a secret from many while wishing you could shout it from the rooftops.

While being pregnant is a time of celebration, some women choose to keep their pregnancy a secret until after the first trimester; especially if they have had previous miscarriages. They don't want to tell everyone that they are pregnant, and later having to share the sad news that they have lost their baby. Even though the happy news is kept a secret, it does not negate the fact that you are pregnant. Jeremiah 1:5 told you that you were pregnant with the Promised Seed of Purpose before you were pregnant.

By this time in your pregnancy, the baby in your uterus is about the size of a lemon, and you cannot keep it a secret any longer. You have a baby bump. That baby on the inside is showing on the outside— now everyone can see! In the spiritual realm, as you are growing spiritually, your Seed of Purpose is also growing. Ephesians 4:15-16 tells us, "Rather, speaking the truth in love, we are to grow up in every way into him who is the head, into Christ, from whom the whole body, joined and held together by every joint with which it is equipped, when each part is working properly, makes the body grow so that it builds itself up in love." God's purposes may be delayed but never denied.

However, the interesting thing is that the purpose is greater than anticipated. It is still being revealed. As I continue with this Promised Seed of Purpose, I realize that one Seed has produced multiple purposes. The pregnancy continues.

7.8 Weeks 18-19: Changing Positions

Wow! You're almost halfway there! You're 18 weeks pregnant, and the baby is as big as an artichoke. However, your uterus is about the size of a cantaloupe. The uterus has grown beyond the capacity of the baby to allow room for the baby to be able to move around more freely.

Time to switch things up! It is around this time that sleeping on your side instead of your back may be a good idea. Another annoyance produces itself. The baby (and your uterus) is getting big enough to press against large veins in the back of your abdomen, which can reduce the amount of blood going to your heart, making you feel lightheaded—or worse, lowering your blood pressure. Sounds scary, but it's totally preventable by just sleeping on your side. In the spiritual pregnancy, sometimes we have to change directions or change positions as the Lord leads. He may have us going in one direction and decide to take us in another direction. We have to be flexible to the move of God. Being flexible will prevent boredom. God is always moving. We must learn to move with Him. Obedience protects the Promised Seed of Purpose. Walking outside of the move of God will produce an Ishmael! Ishmael causes discomfort and trouble. Ask Sarah!

In this stage of your pregnancy, a lot is going on. Not only is your body going through various changes, but the baby in your uterus is going through changes as well. For instance, the baby is working his or her muscles and practicing all kinds of moves. The baby is making some cute little gestures such as yawning, hiccupping, sucking, and swallowing? He or she is twisting, rolling, punching, and kicking too— and is big enough that you might be able to feel him or her doing it! This is an exciting time in your pregnancy.

Be sure in your hectic schedule, that you plan some time to take breaks and unwind. Schedule some "me time" for rest and relaxation. Even God rested after creation. Jesus would take time away from His disciples to spend quality time with God. It is during those times that God will reveal more of Himself and His purpose to you. If one of the definitions of relaxing is "to become less firm," then relaxing our grip on our own lives, careers, families, etc., and giving them over to God in faith is the best way to relax. Relax and enjoy.

At **Week 19,** you still may deal with some of the issues and concerns you had in **Week 18,** but you have learned the formula to work through those annoyances and distractions: "Be careful for nothing; but in everything by prayer and supplication with thanksgiving let your requests be made known unto God. And the peace of God, which passeth all understanding, shall keep your hearts and minds through Christ Jesus" (Philippians 4:6-8).

However, your curiosity is growing stronger! In the natural, some older mothers have said, "you're having a boy because you're carrying the baby low," or, "you're carrying a girl because you're carrying the baby high." In the spiritual, you have sensed God pulling you into areas that you never imagined. Also, you have had a call on your life for years, to fulfill but didn't know exactly what that calling was for sure.

You may have had a strong desire to teach or to work with youth, to open a business, or things of this nature.

Then one day out of nowhere, God sends someone to you to speak a Word over your life that will point you in the direction that you should go or confirm something that you have been hearing in your spirit for a while. That Promised Seed of Purpose has been kicking, turning and hiccupping to let you know that it is there, and it is almost time for the vision to come to fruition.

For those who desire to know the gender of the baby at 19 weeks pregnant, if you take an ultra-sound you will see a lot more than if you are having a boy or girl, you will also see all of baby's body— inside and out. You will be astonished at the development going on in there. Isn't that exciting? During your time of prayer and meditation, God may reveal to you your exact purpose. He will reveal to you just how much your purpose has developed and what the next steps are for you to prepare to bring His purpose to fruition.

7.9 Weeks 20-21: The Half-Way Point

You've made it to the half-way point. **Week 20** of pregnancy! You know what God's purpose is for your life. He has given you direction to move forward in fulfilling the dream or vision that you had years ago. You can name that business or that ministry. Write the vision and make it a plan. Start building your ministry team. Take classes on how to start your dreams. Once God has revealed His purpose and has released you to fulfill that vision, your vision becomes a reality, and you are excited about working the vision.

According to TheBump.com, during this time the doctor will measure fundal height at each prenatal visit. Fundal height is the distance from the pubic bone to the top of your uterus. In centimeters, the fundal height should match your week of pregnancy, give or take two centimeters. So, for example, your 20 weeks pregnant belly should measure around 18 to 22 centimeters. It should continue to increase about a centimeter each week. A higher or lower fundal height could be the sign of a pregnancy condition such as gestational diabetes, a growth issue, or a breech baby, so if it doesn't appear to be average, further testing may be necessary.[18] With each test, there is always the possibility of a distraction of anxiety and fear. But always remember that with every test God makes a way of escape. He has not given us the spirit of fear but of love, power, and a sound mind. Walk in that truth.

Your baby now has working taste buds. He or she is gulping down several ounces of amniotic fluid each day. As you may remember, the amniotic fluid represents the love of God that is surrounding the fetus. In the 20th weeks of pregnancy, in the natural, the baby is gulping down several ounces of this fluid each day.

The Promised Seed of Purpose is ingesting and digesting the love of God which will be the foundation on which the Promised Seed of Purpose is built. Paul states, in I Corinthians 13:1-3, "If I speak in the tongues of men or of angels, but do not have love, I am only a resounding gong or a clanging cymbal. If I have the gift of prophecy and can fathom all mysteries and all knowledge, and if I have a faith that can move mountains, but do not have love, I am nothing. If I give all I possess to the poor and give over my body to hardship that I may boast, but do not have love, I gain nothing." Love covers. Love sustains. Love builds. Love stands firm.

In your detailed 20-week ultrasound, you'll see parts of baby you might not have dreamed possible, including the chambers of his or her heart, the kidneys, and the brain hemispheres. This glimpse into your Purpose that God will reveal to you will provide more detail, and the more you know, the more you are responsible for making sure you bring the Promised Seed of Purpose to fruition. Luke 12:48 says, "...For unto whomsoever much is given, of him shall be much required..."

You are half-way through your pregnancy, and now the pressure is on! Even more, than ever you are excited and anxious. You have found out the gender of your baby, now what? God has revealed your Promised Seed of Purpose, but what do you do now? Psalms 37:23 tells us that "The steps of a good man are ordered by the Lord." God has a plan; therefore, He also has a strategic plan for you to follow. It is not the will of God for you to wander aimlessly through life without a plan or a purpose. God's plan for the Promised Seed of Purpose has been ordered by Him. When we look at the word "ordered" it means to be "established." God tells us in Isaiah 55:11, "So shall My word be that goeth forth out of My mouth: It shall not return unto Me void, but it shall accomplish that which I please, and it shall prosper in the thing whereto I sent it." God's Word concerning your Promised Seed of Purpose has been established, and it shall come to pass.

Since God has revealed His purpose at this point, it is time for you to start to walk in that purpose. Of course, the spiritual steps to take is to stay prayerful and in His Word. But the Bible tells us that faith without works is dead. Your faith needs legs. So, if it is a ministry, a non-profit or a business you are to start, name it. Give that purpose a name. It seems like parents-to-be either come up with baby's name quickly and easily or agonize over it all the way up until the birth. If you haven't picked that perfect name yet, pray and meditate on it. In the meantime, start writing the vision even if you do not have a name for it yet. You'll probably come up with the perfect name once you read the vision and it becomes a reality.

At this stage of your pregnancy, you're not just trying to choose a name for your Promised Seed of Purpose, but you are working on preparing your home for this season. Try not to stress about it. Remember your steps are ordered by the Lord. Follow in His footsteps, and you will not go wrong.

In a natural pregnancy, in **Week 21** your baby is steadily gaining fat to keep warm. The growth rate is slowing down, but its organs are still maturing. "Your baby's oil glands are making a waxy film, called the vernix caseosa, that covers the skin to keep it supple in the amniotic fluid".[19] It is said that the amniotic fluid is the consistency of water. We have heard it said that oil and water will not mix. Oh, but in the spiritual realm, oil and water mix just fine. Think about it. The baby has oil glands!! The baby is in the amniotic fluid, and its skin is covered with this greasy deposit at birth. The amniotic fluid represents the spirit, and the love of God and the oil represents His anointing. The two make a powerful combination. Your Promised Seed of Purpose has oil glands. The oil represents the anointing of God. Your Promised Seed of Purpose has the anointing of God on it before it comes out of your womb. That should make you shout – glory!

As I researched the material for this book, one of the common threads I found was that, throughout pregnancy for many women, there are always annoyances and inconveniences in each stage of pregnancy. Some of these annoyances and inconveniences are recurring, while some are chronic. For instance, here you are in **Week 21** of your pregnancy and you still dealing with stretch marks. However, they are increasing because your uterus is enlarging as the baby continues to grow. Also, other issues arise such as heartburn, dry, itchy skin, your breast may leak, and you begin to have Braxton Hicks. However, while these issues are annoying, some of them serve as indicators of what is happening in the pregnancy. For example, when the breast begins to leak it preparing the milk ducts to be able to nourish your baby. Also, the Braxton Hicks is letting you know that your uterus is practicing for labor. When we are pregnant with the Promised Seed of Purpose, we often get upset and frustrated when we are presented with test and trials. We forget Romans 8:28, that all things are working together for our good. We forget that the trials of our faith worketh patience. We forget 2 Corinthians 4:17 says, "For our light affliction, which is but for a moment, worketh for us a far more exceeding and eternal weight of glory." That far more exceeding eternal weight of glory is the Promised Seed of

Purpose that God has placed in our spirit for His glory.

Some of the things we must endure we may never understand, and we certainly may not like experiencing them. But it may make the process better if we keep our focus on the promised outcome. Remember, at the beginning of your pregnancy, you could look in a mirror, and your body still looks the same. You had not gained any weight. You may have felt a little ill, but the body image was in tack.

However, in **Week 21** of your pregnancy, your body image is entirely different. You may have gained around 13 or more pounds. You have curves in places that were once straight, your breasts are larger which may have you feeling a little sexier and more confident. But the extra weight also might have you feeling…fat. (You're not—you're pregnant!) Remind yourself that you're supposed to be gaining this weight! It's good for you and for baby.

I asked God what does the good weight represent in pregnancy? There is a good amount of weight we are to carry while pregnant and there is a bad amount of weight that we should not carry. The revelation I received is that the good weight is His glory. Throughout the pregnancy in the natural and in the spiritual, we encounter different test and trials. These challenges cannot be avoided, but they can be overcome. Paul tells us in 2 Corinthians 4:17 "For our light affliction, which is but for a moment, worketh for us a far more exceeding and eternal weight of glory…" There is glory in, through and after this pregnancy. "For this cause, we faint not, but though our outward man perishes yet the inward man is renewed day by day." 2 Corinthians 4:16

In a natural pregnancy, just as all the weight you gain during the pregnancy isn't just padding for the baby—it all serves an essential purpose. So, it is with the weight that you gain in your spiritual pregnancy. God's glory surrounding your Promised Seed of Purpose is for a purpose. The weight of God's glory encompasses all that He is and all that He does. In his article, "The Doctrine of Glory" Paul Tripps says:

"You and I are hardwired by God for glory. People are glory-oriented creatures. Animals are not. People are attracted to glorious things, whether it's an exciting drama or sports game, an enthralling piece of music or the best meal ever. Animals live by instinct and exist to survive. We live with a glory hardwiring and chase bigger and better things. God built this glory orientation into us; it's not sinful or against God's will to be attracted to glorious things. Because of this glory orientation, our lives will always be shaped by the pursuit of some kind of glory. You and I will always be chasing something to satisfy the glory hunger that God designed for us to live with."[20]

So, the Promised Seed of Purpose that God has placed in your spirit is designed to carry weight - the weight of His glory! The good weight you are carrying includes the Promised Seed of Purpose, the Holy Spirit, your Spirit, and the Love of God. All those pounds are doing a lot of good, keeping baby alive and healthy—and storing up good stuff to nourish him or her after birth. Anytime you're feeling a little down about your body, think of all the amazing things it's doing!

Now, at 21 weeks, fetal movement is noticeable—, and the baby has reflexes too! If you gently press your palm on your belly, you might feel a little push back. So cool! There continues to be a lot going on in **Week 21**. Your spirit is continuing to increase, and your Promised Seed of Purpose is also growing. You are becoming more sensitive to the movement of what's going on in your spirit. In the natural, the baby's body is preparing to live outside of the womb. It's digestive system preps for the outside world. He or she is manufacturing meconium—the yucky black substance you'll find in the first dirty diaper. Your Promised Seed of Purpose's system is preparing to accept and reject those things that are given to it that may or may not fit into its purpose. There will be some things that you will try to accomplish that may be good ideas but not God ideas and your Promised Seed of Purpose will reject those things that are not God ideas. We must know the difference so that we will not cause a problem with fulfilling our divine purpose.

7.10 Reproduction of Divine Purpose

I am getting excited about this function that takes place in pregnancy. In Genesis, God told Adam and Eve to be fruitful and multiply and replenish the earth. After the flood, He gave Noah the same instructions. In Genesis Chapter One there is a law of God that is stated at least ten times that everything God has created will produce after its own kind. As it is in the natural, so it is in the spirit.

Faith will produce Faith! Hope will produce Hope! Love will produce Love! Success will produce Success! Also, note that you can reproduce negativity during the pregnancy as well. Fear will produce fear. Hate will produce hate.

When God placed the Promised Seed of Purpose in your spirit, it was intended to produce after its own kind. The Promised Seed of Purposed that God has placed in you is not supposed to be a one-time wonder, but it is to reproduce itself. In the natural, while your baby is growing in your womb, its reproductive system is developing too. If it's a girl, she's already has a lifetime supply of eggs in her womb—about six million of them! Having a boy? His testes are still located in his abdomen is where the sperm is produced but will drop in the coming weeks once the scrotum finishes developing. What a mighty God!

This process has no age limit attached to it. If you are 18 and pregnant, 25 and pregnant, 35 and pregnant, 45 and pregnant, 55 and pregnant or 62 and pregnant, your Promised Seed of Purpose is designed to reproduce itself. The dream, that vision, that business, that ministry is supposed to reproduce itself. Your ministry is to beget a ministry. Your business is to beget a business. Reproduction is a part of the divine purpose.

7.11 Week 22: Stretched Into Your Destiny

Whew, everything is growing. Your uterus, the baby, your stomach, your breast, in some cases, your nose, your hair. In **Week 22**, it is getting pretty tight in the uterus. The baby is bigger and seemingly running out of room. In the spirit, you are so filled with anticipation and vision you feel that you are about to burst. But it's not time for delivery yet.

Since the baby is growing and the uterus is reaching capacity, one of the challenges that you may endure during this time is shortness of breath and fatigue. This will require you to change your position when you lie down. When you get weary in the process and feel that you cannot catch your breath remember the "The Spirit of God has made me, And the breath of the Almighty gives me life" (Job 33:4). He will restore your strength.

During this time, the baby's eyes and lips are more developed, he or she's is looking even more like a newborn. The baby is sleeping 12 to 14 hours per day. So, don't panic when you don't feel the baby kicking and moving. Remember that even youths grow tired and weary. I'm not sure what the baby has been doing to get so tired, but it is getting some rest.

Likewise, there will be times when you are working on fulfilling your purpose when rest and quietness are needed. Relish those times, because when the season or time of rest is over, you will have to move forward. The stretching continues. When God is preparing you for the birth of destiny, it seems as if He is stretching you beyond your capacity. Well, He really is stretching you beyond your capacity into a place that He has prepared just for you. It has been said that "Man's extremity is God's opportunity."

Paul's testimony in I Corinthians 1:8-11(MSG) shows us that God will stretch us to the point that we feel as if we want to throw in the towel. Paul had an assignment to go to Asia. Yet even though he was called to this assignment by God, he says, "It was so bad we didn't think we were going to make it. We felt like we'd been sent to death row, that it was all over for us. As it turned out, it was the best thing that could have happened. Instead of trusting in our own strength or wits to get out of it, we were forced to trust God totally— not a bad idea since He's the God who raises the dead! And he did it, rescued us from certain doom. And he'll do it again, rescuing us as many times as we need rescuing…"

God will stretch us into our destiny and protect us in the process. Remember, the Promised Seed of Purpose is growing and stretching. So, your spirit is also stretching for your good. It's like exercise—the more you stretch your muscles, the stronger you become. This stretching has a purpose. The more God stretches you, He is enlarging your capacity to hold more of His power, wisdom, more understanding of who He is and what His purpose is for your life and the life of the Promised Seed of Purpose growing in your womb. When He increases your capacity to carry more of His glory, He will increase your influence with Him and man.

There's a blessing in the stretching. Isaiah 54:2-3 says, "Enlarge the place of your tent, and let them stretch out the curtains of your dwellings; Do not spare; lengthen your cords and strengthen your stakes. For you shall expand to the right and to the left, and your descendants will inherit the nations, and make the desolate cities inhabited…"

Your stretching is not just for you, but for generations to come. It comes with a promise. Isaiah continues by saying "Behold, I have created the blacksmith who blows the coals in the fire, who brings forth an instrument for his work; And I have created the spoiler to destroy.

No weapon formed against you shall prosper, and every tongue which rises against you in judgment you shall condemn. This is the heritage of the servants of the Lord, and their righteousness is from Me…" (Isaiah 54:16-17). Remember, there is purpose in the stretching.

7.12 Week 23: Write the Vision and Make it Plain

We have now reached **Week 23.** Your baby's skin is still wrinkled because your baby still has more weight to gain. Your Promised Seed of Purpose still has more of the glory of God to be revealed in it. It does not appear what it shall be—but when Christ reveals the total purpose—and you walk in His purpose, the weight of the glory of God on the Promised Seed of Purpose will cause the wrinkles to disappear. Also, the fine hair that is now on the baby's body sometimes turns darker. It has been said that hair symbolizes physical strength. Some believe that you can tell if a person is healthy by the quality of hair and nails.

When I was younger, my mother took me to see an older doctor who then was in her 80's. She looked at my hands and squeezed my fingernails to determine if I had a deficiency of some sort. The Promised Seed of Purpose you are carrying is being equipped to fulfill its purpose. That's why it is imperative that we who are pregnant with the Promised Seed of Purpose speak life over the seed, eat properly by not allowing all manner of thoughts and words to seep into our spirit.

At 23 weeks pregnant, the baby's getting ready for his or her big debut by listening in on what's going on in the outside world. The baby's entertaining him- or herself by listening to your voice and your heartbeat and can even hear some loud sounds like cars honking and dogs barking. Watch what you say, and what is being said around you.

In the natural, while the baby is preparing for its entrance into the world, you're getting ready too. Just remember while having the nursery painted and stocked with diapers is important, there are less fun things you should have on your radar, namely, financials. It has been said that during this time it is a good idea for the parents-to-be to consider making financial decisions such as calling your health insurance company to make sure that you are covered, and if any changes need to be made. Every couple should have a will in place.

Likewise, once God has revealed to you that it is time to bring forth the vision of the Promised Seed of Purpose, you must begin "writing" the vision and making it plain. As the Lord told Habakkuk: "Write down the revelation and make it plain on tablets so that a herald may run with it. For the revelation awaits an appointed time; it speaks of the end and will not prove false. Though it lingers, wait for it; it will certainly come and will not delay" Habakkuk 2:2-3 (NIV). In other words, write while you wait. Go get your business license, get your 501(c)(3) established, get your Employer Identification Number (EIN). Go look for a location for your business. Get your business plan in place. Get your business logo and cards designed and printed. In other words, prepare for the birth of your Promised Seed of Purpose. We serve a prepared God who wants a prepared person.

Even though you are over half-way through your pregnancy, please know that the enemy will always try to cause you to panic. It is not uncommon for there to be a vaginal discharge during this time in your pregnancy. It is nothing to fear even if there is an odor or discoloration. Go to see your OB/GYN for him to give you something for the infection. In the spiritual, it is called a distraction. Don't panic. Go to God in prayer and let Him handle your problems. Remember, cast all your cares (distractions) on Him for He cares for you. He wants the Promised Seed of Purpose to be birthed for His glory.

Other than that, enjoy a little time off from all the poking, prodding, and peeing in a cup. You're seeing your OB only once a month right now so you may not have a doctor's appointment or ultrasound. You may be done with your genetic testing. As it is in the natural, so it is in the spiritual. God does not allow us to be tested all the time. In Psalms 30:5, He promised that "weeping may endure for a night, but joy comes in the morning." Tests in pregnancy are necessary, and tests in spiritual pregnancy are also necessary. It is during the tests we come to realize how much we must depend on God.

In the third trimester, you'll be busier with appointments, like seeing your doctor every other week. You may not feel as energetic as you do now—so use this time to get stuff done and out of the way!

7.13 Weeks 24-25: The Heartbeat of Your Purpose

In **Week 24**, not much has changed with you. Your stomach is still stretching, you're gaining a few pounds. Your feet may or may not be a little swollen. But everything is going well. However, what you do not see is what is happening on the inside. Your baby is starting to make white blood cells, which will help it fight off disease and infection.

The baby is developing fighting defenses. The Promised Seed of Purpose is infused with the anointing of God and covered by the blood of Jesus to withstand anything that the enemy throws its way to thwart its purpose. Remember the hair represents strength, the oil represents the anointing, and amniotic fluid represents the love of God. The Promised Seed of Purpose is undefeatable, unconquerable and victorious!

God placed in your spirit destiny before you were born. It was already determined that you were to be a winner. Pregnancy in the spiritual realm is a little different than a natural pregnancy. In the natural, it takes nine months for a baby to develop and be birthed. However, in the spiritual realm, it can be shorter or longer. But whether it is a short pregnancy or a longer pregnancy, there is a promise attached to you and your Seed that says: "...And he shall be like a tree planted by the rivers of water, that bringeth forth his fruit in his season; his leaf also shall not wither; and whatsoever he doeth shall prosper" (Psalms 1:3). Your destiny is about to be fulfilled, no matter how long it takes! Your age doesn't matter to God. Your purpose does. He needs you to give birth!

In **Week 25**, you can hear the heartbeat through a stethoscope or, depending on the position of the baby, by others putting an ear against your belly. Others at this point can begin to hear evidence of what is going on the inside of your womb. Purpose has a sound. There's a steady heartbeat in purpose. That heartbeat lets you know, and others know that while the vision has not come to fruition, it is still alive and well. If, in your mind, you are older and seemingly past your prime, remember that God holds eternity in His hands, and time has no effect on Him fulfilling His purpose through you. "For the vision is yet for an appointed time, but at the end it shall speak, and not lie: though it tarry, wait for it; because it will surely come, it will not tarry" (Habakkuk 2:3). When it is time for purpose to break through the womb of your spirit - get in position because it's coming!

Besides, in the natural the baby is still growing and moving, your uterus is growing upward. In the spiritual, while your Promised Seed of Purpose is growing and maturing inside your spirit, your spirit is also shifting upward. Your mindset is changing as you prepare to give birth to the Promise. You are growing in the grace and knowledge of the Lord. This is causing a shift in your walk with God. You may still have distractions in this season, but because your spirit has shifted upward, the distractions don't affect you as they used to at the beginning of your pregnancy. You must learn to bask in the presence of the Lord to soothe those annoyances and distractions. You have learned how to move from stressful situations and allow the Lord to handle the issues. You are too close to turn around and to allow anything or anyone to thwart this pregnancy. You're moving forward toward delivery.

7.14 Weeks 26-27: Moving to the Right Drum Beat

In **Week 26**, your baby's hearing is fully developed. As the baby reacts to sounds, its pulse increases. In the spirit, your Promised Seed of Purpose can hear every word spoken, every sound that is made. There will be sounds that will make your baby leap. Often times your baby will move in your spirit while you are sitting in anointed surroundings. Be aware of who is around you and what is spoken to you and around you. Remember, your Promised Seed of Purpose can hear. Even the music you listen to must be good for the spirit. In the natural, your baby will even move to the rhythm of the music. In the spirit, make sure that your Promised Seed of Purpose is moving to the right drumbeat.

Additionally, the baby's lungs are still growing but are not yet mature. Clean air is important for the baby inside the womb. Whatever you breathe in affects the baby. You are carrying the Promised Seed of Purpose, and everything you do will have an effect on you carrying this Seed to full-term. So be cognizant of what you hear, see, eat, and breathe into your spirit.

The baby's constant movements should be reassuring. God will allow your Seed to move in your spirit as a reminder that you are about to give birth to your Promise. In Genesis, God promised Abraham that he was going to be the father of many nations. However, He did not tell him just once, but He reminded him 4 times of the Promise. It was 10 years between the initial promise and the first reminder. Like all of us, I am sure Abraham was wondering if he heard God or was this wishful thinking on his part. He was 75 when the promise was given, and now, he's 85 and no baby! God doesn't move in our time but in His timing. God again reminded Abraham twice more of the promise. He allowed the Promised Seed of Purpose to move in the womb of Abraham as a reminder of what He had promised.

In a natural pregnancy, there may be some rib pain as your baby grows and pushes upward on your rib cage. The pressure may also be causing indigestion and heartburn. You may also feel stitch-like pains down the sides of your abdomen as your uterine muscle stretches. As in the spiritual, your Promised Seed of Purpose is getting larger, the vision is getting clearer, your spirit is moving upward, and you're being stretched causing a little discomfort. Giving birth to a business, ministry, organization, or a natural baby will cause discomfort. But know that there is purpose in the discomfort. Greater is coming!

In 13 weeks, the baby will be brought into the world. Here in **Week 27**, in the natural the baby's hands are active. In the spirit, hands have great significance. For instance, each hand has a unique identity. No two sets of fingerprints are the same. The baby has an identity that only he or she has. The same in the spiritual realm. God has given each of us various gifts and assignments that no one can accomplish but us. Paul tells us in I Corinthians 12:4-11:

"There are diversities of gifts, but the same Spirit. There are differences of ministries, but the same Lord. And there are diversities of activities, but it is the same God who works all in all. But the manifestation of the Spirit is given to each one for the profit of all: for to one is given the word of wisdom through the Spirit, to another the word of knowledge through the same Spirit, to another faith by the same Spirit, to another gifts of healings by the same Spirit, to another the working of miracles, to another prophecy, to another discerning of spirits, to another different kinds of tongues, to another the interpretation of tongues. But one and the same Spirit works all these things, distributing to each one individually as He wills."

Abraham tried to give the identity that was assigned to Isaac to Ishmael. The Promised Seed of Purpose growing inside of your spirit is given to you to birth, not Hagar. You may have felt that someone else can do what you have had in your spirit to do because it's too late for you to do it. You may feel incompetent and unqualified. But look yourself in the mirror and say, "I can do this with the help of the Lord." You have the best OB/GYN to help you give birth to the Promised Seed of Purpose. Keep it going! You're almost there.

Chapter 8:
The Third
Trimester

8.1 Week 28: Rest on What You Know

If you're anything like me, three months always sounds better than thirteen weeks. So, when I was six months pregnant, I didn't count my pregnancy in terms of weeks. In my sixth month, I was so excited I wanted to know what I was carrying. I was listening to the mothers of the church who said, "You're carrying high, so it's a girl, or you're carrying low, so it's a boy." But I really wanted to know for sure. Even though I wanted to know, I wanted to be surprised the day of the birth. One thing was for sure, I was pregnant, the baby was doing well, and so was I. When you're pregnant, you cannot carry around a portable sonogram to keep track of how the baby is growing and to see how and what the baby is doing. However, medical science gives us a glimpse at what is going on inside the womb.

In the natural, the baby has grown to about 15.75 inches from head to toe. Brain waves show rapid eye movement (REM) sleep, which means your baby may be dreaming. Earlier in **Week 22**, we said that God commanded Adam and Eve to produce after their own kind. We also said that the Promised Seed of Purpose is to produce after its own kind. Your Promised Seed of Purpose is to reproduce itself. That means that your Promised Seed of Purpose must be creative and have ideas, dreams, and visions. So, while still in the womb, the seeds that are already planted in the fetus is dreaming of what it can produce after it is birthed. Whew! Your Promise Seed of Purpose is dreaming about what it will become. Eyelids of a natural baby are opening at this stage. Could it be that the Promised Seed of Purposes' dreams are so real that it is opening his or her eyes to see if the dream is actually happening?

In a natural pregnancy, many women experience swollen feet, have trouble sleeping and breathing, and having to urinate more often. The same irritations happened in a spiritual pregnancy. Please know that as you get closer to delivery, the enemy will do his best to try to discourage you, make you fearful, frustrated, disgusted, and busted. There will be times when you just want to give up because of the annoyances that keep popping up in your life. This is the time to rest on what you know. You know that your OB/GYN (Jesus) is with you every step of the way. You're about to give birth in a few more weeks. Stay focused and keeping moving.

8.2 Weeks 29-31: God Still Moves

In **Week 29**, a baby's eyes are almost always blue and can distinguish bright sunlight or artificial light through the uterine wall. The baby is performing fewer acrobatics as conditions in the womb become more cramped, but he's still doing a lot of kicking and stretching.

In the spiritual, God has given the Promised Seed of Purpose eyesight that is affected by external conditions. There will be times that you're in a situation or an environment that is not conducive for your Promised Seed of Purpose being exposed. In the spirit, it is rejecting the intrusive object that is obstructing its sight. Because it has grown it cannot turn away as fast as it once did when it was smaller. It will send a signal that this situation is not good by kicking or stretching and may make you uncomfortable thus causing you to remove yourself from the situation.

When it comes to giving birth to a Promised Seed of Purpose, there are always hindrances. When destiny is before you, and your purpose is about to be fulfilled, expect the enemy to come and cause problems—things that will actually cause your blood to boil or rise. You may lose your job, your spouse and children may start acting crazy, your money starts to act funny, etc. Go to your OB/GYN, Jesus. He has the prescription to handle these issues as well.

At **Week 30**, the baby continues to grow at a normal rate. Eyebrows and eyelashes are fully developed, and hair on the head is getting thicker. Head and body are now proportioned like a newborn. Hands are now fully formed, and fingernails are growing. In other words, the baby is taking shape. If a sonogram was taken at this stage of pregnancy, you could probably tell who the baby will look like mommy or daddy.

In **Week 30**, your Promised Seed of Purpose has matured and has its own identity. Your spirit is continuing to be lifted as the Promised Seed of Purpose grows and matures. You're getting even more excited because you have been feeding and nurturing this Seed, and you are close to delivery. You may feel that you are ready to give birth now, but you still have about 10 weeks to go. You are consistently receiving nudges from the Promised Seed of Purpose to let you know that the Promise is still yea and amen.

It is also at this stage that your Promised Seed of Purpose may change positions frequently and respond to stimuli, including sound, pain, and light. Even though your Promised Seed of Purpose is still growing, always be open to change. God still moves, and while He may have given you a vision to start a ministry for homeless women, He at any time can have the Promised Seed of Purpose to change positions and take it another step further. It's your vision, but it's for God purpose.

I have always been taught that when God wants to get His point across, He says something more than once. We see it in the case of Abraham. He reminded Abraham four times that he was going to be a father of many nations. He tells us in His Word in Isaiah 43:26, "Put Me in remembrance…" It's not that God forgets His Word. He already knows what He has said, but He wants to make sure that you remember what He said.

Throughout the pregnancy there seem to be times of discomfort. These are occurrences of distractions and frustrations that come to take us off track. However, we must stay focused and determined to give birth to the Promised Seed of Purpose no matter what happens.

In **Week 31**, and as a reminder, your baby can hear distinct sounds, including familiar voices and music. Be aware of what you are listening to and what you are allowing to enter your spirit. Your Promised Seed of Purpose resides there. It is hearing everything that is being said and going into your spirit. In natural birth, it is recommended that women began practicing their breathing and relaxation exercises in preparation for the delivery. Nine weeks and counting.

8.3 Weeks 32-33: In Stillness: God Is Up to Something

While you cannot see it, the baby fills almost all of the space in your uterus now— but may still have enough room to do somersaults. A layer of fat is forming under your baby's skin. The baby is practicing opening his eyes and breathing. In the spiritual realm, the Promised Seed of Purpose is growing and maturing. There are times when the movement in your spirit is so strong that you want to praise God in a loud voice. What is going on inside is so powerful that it is getting harder to contain. There are times when God is about to do something great in your life you want to tell everyone. But there are times that you must contain your excitement. Like Mary, some things you must ponder in your heart.

In a natural pregnancy, this is when you would probably start seeing your OB/GYN more frequently. Likewise, in the spiritual realm, as you get closer to delivering your Promised Seed of Purpose, you may increase your time of devotion and intimacy with God. This may be a good time to start lining up your midwives to pray with you and to encourage you until you give birth.

Week 33 does not bring any significant changes that can be seen from the outside. However, in the next few weeks, the baby will have a growth spurt. Your baby begins to move less now as it runs out of room and curls up with knees bent, chin resting on chest, and arms and legs crossed. Even though the baby is not moving as much, there is still a heartbeat, and there is still movement. There are times in our spiritual walk when it seems as if there's no movement. Nothing is happening. You may see a glimmer of light and feel a flutter of something moving, but everything seems to be at a standstill. When we think that God is not doing anything that means that He's up to something and He needs you still and rested. It's time to bring the purpose to fruition. So, when the Promised Seed of Purpose is quiet, rest in the fact that God is up to something. Count Down! 7 Weeks and counting!

8.4 Weeks 34-35: Sow, Nurture and Produce

By **Week 34,** the baby is settling into the head-down position, although it might not be final. This is the position you would want the baby to be in the when it is time to deliver. If the baby is poised in the wrong position, it can stop the birthing process. The baby's head must be tucked down so that the head comes out first. If the baby holds its head in an odd position, problems can result.

The same holds true in your spiritual pregnancy. The Promised Seed of Purpose must be in the right position for it to be birthed without complications. The position of the head often expresses an attitude or emotion. That seed that you have been nurturing for the past 33 weeks must have a posture of humility. Remember, what you sow and nurture you will produce. If you are mean and arrogant, your seed will inherit the traits of its carrier.

Have you ever heard of pregnant women who were mean and nasty during their pregnancy and when they had their children the children had the same attitude that their mother displayed during her pregnancy? I have seen women who cried and were emotional almost their entire pregnancy. When the baby was born, it seemed always to cry.

In an article written by James Goodlatte entitled, "A Mother's Emotions Affect Her Unborn Child," he states that "Experts and evidence suggest that positive thinking can shape the body, heal internally, and even nurture a healthier child during pregnancy. A pregnant woman's thoughts have a physical connection to her unborn child." In his article, he quotes Dr. Thomas Verny, who said, "Everything the pregnant mother feels, and thinks is communicated through neurohormones to her unborn child, just as surely as are alcohol and nicotine."[21]

So, it is crucial that you as the carrier of the Promised Seed of Purpose have a mind transformation that lines up with the Word and purpose of God for the Promised Seed of Purpose. If the head is not in its right position, it will affect the birthing and the outcome of the birth.

At this stage, except for the lungs, all of the baby's organs are almost fully mature. Your Promised Seed of Purpose is developing internally for it be able to flourish after you give birth.

Your uterus (spirit) hardens and contracts as practice for labor, known as Braxton Hicks contractions, but you may not feel them yet. Your spirit is even preparing for the birth of the Promised Seed of Purpose. It has been developing over the past 33 weeks, and now your spirit is preparing itself for the birth. Your pelvis has expanded and may ache, especially at the back. The Promised Seed of Purpose is preparing itself for this blessed delivery. Get ready—the Promise is Coming! Six weeks and counting!

8.5 Weeks 35-36: Are you Ready to Deliver?

In the natural, at this stage, your baby's lungs are almost fully developed. It's still building fat deposits beneath its skin to keep warm after it leaves your womb. God is insulating your Promised Seed of Purpose to enter a new dimension that it has never experienced. YOU are about to embark into a new realm that you have never experienced. You are about to give birth to your vision, your dream, your purpose. Stay close to God in this season because you do not want to misstep and cause the Promise to be delivered before its time.

You have been carrying and nurturing this Promised Seed of Purpose but are you ready for its delivery? Are you positioning yourself to give birth to this seed? Have you taken the necessary steps to make it happen? For instance, have you started writing your book? Do you have a manuscript? Have you obtained your 501(c)(3) to start your non-profit? Have you purchased your passport to travel out of the country? Have you taken the necessary classes to be qualified for your dream job? Have you completed the required paperwork to start your ministry? Are you prepared to give birth to your Promised Seed of Purpose? You are about to give birth! 5 weeks and counting!

You are now **36 weeks** and almost at the finish line. The baby may drop lower in your abdomen. You are hopeful that the baby is in a head-down position in preparation for the birth. Your Promised Seed of Purpose is now in position and just waiting for due season to arrive. You are still getting reminders that the Promise is alive and well. You get a kick or a contraction to let you know that you are closer to delivery. Your uterus (spirit) has grown bigger in faith and excitement for what is about to happen. You may have been waiting for years for this dream or vision to come to pass, but now the due date is right upon you. Your soul is excited and overwhelmed with joy. In addition, your faith capacity has been enlarged. As you build up your most holy faith, it enlarges your capacity to be able to fulfill your purpose. But you're in the home stretch!

As you get closer to deliver you may feel fatigued for one hour and get a burst of energy in the next hour. Your back may ache, and you may even feel discomfort in your buttocks and pelvis. I must say, as I write, I feel these symptoms. I have been pregnant with this book for over 15 years. My Promised Seed of Purpose has been kicking me in my ribs for the past two months to get ready to deliver this baby! My back is hurt, my head hurt, even my buttocks hurt! But I had to push past these annoyances to give birth! You may feel the same way. But you are too close to quit—four weeks to go!

8.6 Weeks 37-38: Expect Pressure

In **Weeks 37-38** your baby's head is usually positioned down into the pelvis by now, and you're feeling pressure. When God has a purpose on your life, there will be seasons of pressure. The Seed that you are carrying is not just an idea or vision that you came up with. We serve a creative God. He gives those He has made in His image ideas to produce things in the earth realm for His glory.

The Promised Seed of Purpose that you are carrying when submitted to God will have an anointing placed on it. To get oil (which represents the anointing), there must be pressure put on the seed to get the oil. So, expect the pressure because God is getting the anointing out of your Promised Seed of Purpose. NEWS FLASH! We often think of the use of the olive when we speak about getting oil, but I found out that there are seeds that produce oil as well. Your Promised Seed of Purpose will produce oil!

At this point, you are about 3 weeks away from giving birth. It is always a possibility that the baby can come early. According to WebMD.com, "95% of all babies are born within two weeks of their mother's due date."[22] We know that God works with timing more than time. Even though your Promised Seed of Purpose was scheduled to be delivered on your set time; God's timing may change your schedule. We may not understand the timing of God, but we can rest assured that His timing is perfect. He's never too early, nor is He never too late. Often because we do not understand the timing of God, we get frustrated in the wait or even when God allows certain things to happen in our lives. "But know that His way is perfect; the word of the Lord proves true…" (Psalm 18:30). Trust His timing and be ready if He chooses to speed up your delivery. The baby is in position - 3 weeks and counting!

8.7 Weeks 39-40: Guard Your Purpose

At **39-40 weeks**, you have protected and nurtured your Promised Seed of Purpose up to this point, and it continues as you provide antibodies to protect it from illness. According to an article by Health Direct - How Your Baby's Immune System Develops, "Antibodies are passed from mother to baby through the placenta during the last three months of pregnancy. This gives the baby some protection when they are born. The placenta not only provides the baby the oxygen and nutrients throughout the pregnancy, but it also provides protection against illness for when the baby arrives."[23]

Let's convert this exchange to the spiritual realm. The Promised Seed of Purpose is being provided with the necessary protection to flourish and be healthy when it is birthed by the Holy Spirit. Throughout your pregnancy you have not walked in the counsel of the wicked, neither did you stand in the way of sinners, or sit in the seat of scoffers; but your delight has been in the law of the Lord, and you have learned to meditate on His law - day and night. Therefore, you have been like a tree planted by streams of water and is about to yield your fruit in its season... Now, all that you do will prosper" (Paraphrased Psalm 1:1-3 - KJV). These antibodies help to build the colony of bacteria in the gut that contributes to their immunity. In other words, The Holy Spirit is able to guard what you have entrusted to him.

These last two weeks are both exciting and exhausting. Some of you have been waiting for years for this moment to come. Now that it is almost here, you're excited and even a little apprehensive.

In the natural, the baby's head has dropped into the mother's pelvis—a head-down position lets you breathe a little easier. Your Promised Seed of Purpose is in position, and you're feeling the pressure. In natural pregnancies, this is the time that many women want the pregnancy to be over already! You are anxious to see your Promised Seed of Purpose!

Your body has already started preparing for the birth. Your pelvis is widening, the baby's head is in the downward position, and you have been feeling false labor pains.

When I was pregnant with my first child, I had no point of reference for being pregnant. There were times I thought I was in labor, only to find out, no, not yet! While I loved being pregnant, I was anxious to see if I was having a girl or a boy.

When the real labor began, I could definitely tell the difference! I remember being in labor for so long, and the pain was so great, that I asked God to forgive me of my sins and to take me home. I was ready to die. I wanted to give up before the Promise. I'm glad that God did not listen to me. I would not have seen my beautiful baby daughter Chanette Ome'ga. I called her muffin—and she's still my muffin.

Everyone's labor experience is different. Some women have back labor, and some do not. Some have short labor, and some like in my case have long labor. Nevertheless, we all had to labor to bring forth our little bundles of joy. In giving birth in the natural as well as the spiritual to the Promised Seed of Purpose, there will be labor pain. But there is purpose in the pain. The pressure you feel is letting you know that it's almost time. You're down to the wire—with one week and counting!

Your Promised Seed of Purpose is almost here. In a natural birth, it is not uncommon for the first baby to be late. But in this spiritual birth, God has said, you have waited long enough. Your wait is over! Your season has come! You may be a little afraid to step out, but you are at a place in your pregnancy that you have to PUSH! God has impregnated you with the Promised Seed of Purpose for His Glory. All of the pressure you are feeling and all of the discomfort you are experiencing is for His glory. He wants to use the vision, the dream, the desire that He has placed in you to bring forth in the earth to show to the world who He is.

The Bible says, "being confident of this very thing, that he which hath begun a good work in you will perform it until the day of Jesus Christ…" (Philippians 1:6 KJV). What God has started; He will finish. It's almost time! Birth should happen any day now! You may find yourself nesting. Nesting is when you may wake up one morning feeling full of energy and start to clean and organize your entire house, go shopping as I did when I was pregnant with my son Josh. I thought I had Braxton Hicks, but I wanted to go grocery shopping. By the way, I was actually in the beginning stages of labor. I had Josh the very next day.

God has already determined that you will give birth in your 40th week. You are feeling the labor pains. It's time! Get in position and get ready to push out your long-awaited Promised Seed of Purpose.

Whew!! You've made it!

Chapter 9:
Labor, Delivery,
& Life After Birth

9.1 The Birthing Room

You have made it to the birthing room, and everything is in place. The OB/GYN and assistants have the instruments to ensure a smooth delivery. Remember, God has already told you that you will give birth to the Promised Seed of Purpose. You can stand on that promise alone.

If this is your first baby, you really have no frame of reference for the pain that you are about to endure. I remember asking my mother, "Mom, does it hurt to have a baby?" Her response to me was, "It's not too bad." She was so wrong! But even if she told me that it was really painful, it was something that I had to experience in order to know. What others may say to you about giving birth to the Promised Seed of Purpose may vary, but you and only you have to go through the process of this pain.

In a natural pregnancy, at the beginning of labor, the cervix starts to soften so it can open. This is called the latent phase, and you may feel irregular contractions. The pain is not intense at this point. It is only when established labor begins that your pain increases. At this point your cervix has dilated to more than three centimeters and regular contractions have begun to open your cervix.

In the spiritual, the beginning of your labor pains of may be the challenges you are having in starting your ministry, business, etc. You may come up against opposition that may cause you to cry out to God in frustration. The pain of frustration is real, but not to the point where you want to give up. You know that you are about give birth to the Promise.

In a natural pregnancy, labor can be slow. If your contractions aren't coming often enough or aren't strong enough, or if your baby is in an awkward position, the OB/GYN may consider breaking your water. Remember, God has already established that this labor will not be long, so the breaking of your water will be necessary. Without it, you would get stuck. You wouldn't see the fullness of what He has in store. The amniotic fluid represents the spirit of God and the love of God. When the water breaks, there's no turning back. Your pain may increase. You are facing some things that you never expected—like being laid off from your job, a break in a relationship, an illness, etc. It's easy to get discouraged and begin doubting that you are going to give birth to the Promise. But I challenge you to renew and transform your thinking. Take a new perspective on the issue: the water breaking is a sign you're about to give birth. God is about to do something new.

There are rivers in the desert (IS. 43:19). The Promised Seed of Purpose that you have been carrying is about to break forth. The Spirit of God is going to release it into the earth to be used for His glory. This Promised Seed of Purpose, when submitted to God, will water the earth with His glory. "Those areas that have been barren will begin to bring forth life. Those dry places will now have springs of water" (Isaiah 41:18-20). In the Passion Translation it says: "I will open up refreshing streams on the barren hills and springing fountains in the valleys. I will make the desert a pleasant pool, and the dry land springs of water." Your labor has intensified, and you have gone from three centimeters to eight. When you are about to give birth, the pain for birthing intensifies. Things in your life seem to start going awry. People start acting as if they have lost their minds. The money is funny. You are turned down for a business loan. You can't find people to work for you or help you, you get laid off, etc.

When I was pregnant with my daughter, I went into the hospital because I had developed an umbilical hernia that was hurting terribly every time she would move. When I went into the hospital and they examined me, they told me that I was four centimeters and I would not be going home. I asked the nurse, "is this all the pain I will have while in labor?" She told me, "Not much more than that." Well that was not the truth! By the time I reached seven centimeters, I was praying to die. The labor intensified. I was in labor for 18 hours. 18 hours!

When you are birthing the Promised Seed of Purpose, you will have birthing pain. But remember that God has prepared you for this. Everything that you have gone through leading up to this blessed event has prepared you to give birth to your Promised Seed of Purpose. This whole process began in the mind of God and will end with purpose being fulfilled. God has brought you to this place and in this time to bring to fruition the Promised Seed of Purpose that He purposed for your life before you were conceived. You cannot be pregnant forever. You must give birth. Isaiah 66:9 (NIV) Do I bring to the moment of birth and not give delivery?" says the Lord. "Do I close up the womb when I bring to delivery?" says your God. Trust God to bring forth the vision. It has been said that God will not position us for greatness without preparing us for destiny. He will position us to fulfill what He has placed in our spirit. If we submit that vision to Him, He will help us to see it come to fruition.

It is in the time of labor that we travail. Travailing is a time to engage in painful or laborious effort. Giving birth to the Promised Seed of Purpose may be a time of travailing. In a natural birth, the baby must come through the birth canal. It is a tight space that the baby must pass through. There will be pressure on you and the baby. In the spirit, this pressure is preparing for the birth of the Promised Seed of Purpose. The labor pains represent the tests and trials you will endure by bringing something into the world that will bring glory to God. The enemy will fight tooth and nail to try to make you give up.

There will be tests. There will be struggles. There will be doubts. There will be fears. But just as laborious as these issues are that are causing us to travail as we push to our destiny, we also must press into God in prayer even the more.

It may require travailing in prayer—crying out to God in those times of pain and suffering, and those times of fear and doubt. Remember, in order to get oil from a seed, pressure must be applied. The healthier oils come from seeds. So, know that even though you are having to go through the pressure of pushing out this Promised Seed of Purpose, your purpose is being fulfilled for the glory of God!

9.2 The Delivery

I remember when I was giving birth to my children, when I had a contraction, the doctor would say PUSH! I was in pain, I didn't feel like pushing, and I wanted the pain to go away. If I wanted the pain to go away, and if I wanted to see my baby, I had to push past the pain.

In a natural pregnancy, you can push while squatting, sitting, kneeling—even on your hands and knees. During your time of travailing in prayer to push out your Promised Seed of Purpose, **your position does not matter**. You are about to give birth to the Promised Seed of Purpose! It is painful and it does not feel good. But you must push past the pain and focus of the Promise. Cry out to God on your knees, on your back, squatting, or sitting. Remember, "He is your refuge and strength; a very present help in the time of trouble" (Psalms 46:1).

Don't give up now! Your Promised Seed of Purpose head is crowning. You can see the fruit of your labor. You can even feel it. PUSH! There it is! The umbilical cord that was used to nourish your Promised Seed of Purpose has been cut.

9.3 The Next Steps

Now what? Even though you nurtured the Promised Seed of Purpose in your womb while you carried it, nurturing does not end after you give birth. You must continue to nurture the baby after it is born. After the vision has come to fruition, you must work with it. It is still an infant. You have nurture it until it is mature enough to reproduce itself. In order to be prepared to nourish your Promised Seed of Purpose when it is born, make sure that you apply Jude 1:20-22 (KJV): "But ye,

beloved, building up yourselves on your most holy faith, praying in the Holy Ghost, keep yourselves in the love of God, looking for the mercy..."
Like most new parents, we can be clueless on how to handle a baby. We must be taught the right and wrong way to take care of new life. The same with the Promised Seed of Purpose. You must be directed by the Holy Spirit to care for what you have just birthed. Your Promised Seed of Purpose requires special care. Here as some practical ways in caring for the Promised Seed of Purpose:

1. **Prayer**: "Pray without ceasing" (I Thessalonians 5:17). As a newborn baby should be covered, so should the Promised Seed of Purpose. Cover your Promised Seed of Purpose with prayer.

2. **Feed the Seed**: 1 Peter 2:2 - Like newborn babies, crave pure spiritual milk, so that by it you may grow up in your salvation. Your seed came out a baby, but God wants to bring your vision and dreams to maturity. When a baby is not properly nourished it will not grow.

3. **Speak Life Over Your Seed:** (Proverbs 18:21) says, "death and life are in the power of the tongue: and they that love it shall eat the fruit thereof. Even in times of frustration speak life."

4. **Protect Your Seed from An Unhealthy Environment:** Everyone cannot handle your Seed. Toxic people should not be allowed to handle your Seed. Just as newborn babies can pick-up the spirit of those who they feel are toxic, you should be wary of who you allow around your Promised Seed of Purpose. Negativity is poisonous to you and your Promised Seed of Purpose.

5. **Create a Soothing Atmosphere Conducive to Growth:** "In thy presence is fullness of joy; at thy right hand there are pleasures for

evermore" (Psalm 16:11). You have given birth to the Promised Seed of Purpose, now God is calling you to nurture the Seed and to go higher! We must lay aside those things that will hinder us from fulfilling our purpose. "Let us lay aside every weight, and the sin which doth so easily beset us, and let us run with patience the race that is set before us. Looking unto Jesus the author and finisher of our faith" (Hebrew 12:1-2).

9.4 Purpose Begets Purpose

The Bible says that "Every good and perfect gift comes from above" (James 1:17). However, He did not give gifts for no reason. There is purpose attached to each gift, talent, vision, and dream that He has given. The Promised Seed of Purpose was placed in your spirit so that it can be used, so that His will may be done on Earth as it is in Heaven. He wants His glory revealed on the Earth. "For in Him all things were created: things in heaven and on earth, visible and invisible, whether thrones or powers or rulers or authorities; all things have been created through him and for him" (Colossians 1:16).

What is purpose? It is the reason for which something is done or created or for which something exists. Your Seed has PURPOSE! There is a purpose for the business that you want to start. There is a purpose for the ministry you want to start. There is a purpose for the music and poetry you have been writing. There is purpose for the family you desire to have one day. According to T.D. Jakes, "If you can't figure out your purpose, figure out your passion. For your passion will lead you right into your purpose."24 There is no good thing that He will withhold from them who walks upright before Him. (Psalms 84:11). Fulfilling your purpose is a GOOD THING!

God had you in mind before you were formed in your mother's womb. He ordained your purpose before you were conceived, and it is through an active, intimate relationship with God where Hope (egg) and Faith (sperm) are lovingly caressed and quickened by the Holy Spirit to grow and mature from an embryonic seed to a promised fulfilled. The Promised Seed of Purpose at it very core in each one of us and is intended to establish the Kingdom of God on Earth, as Jesus teaches us in the Lord's Prayer, "thy kingdom come, thy will be done, on Earth as it is in Heaven." Birthing of the Promised Seed of Purpose enables each one of us to do our part for the Kingdom, and ushers in the glory of God on Earth for all to witness. This is promise fulfilled!

One may ask, how about all the talented people who are doing great things; did God impregnate them with a Promised Seed of Purpose? Remember, every good and perfect gift comes from above also, gifts come without repentance. God has gifted many with amazing talents that are not being used for His glory—but that was the intent.

God revealed this last thing as I am closing out this book. Just as there was purpose in Sarah giving birth to Isaac at the age of 89— showing that with God, nothing is impossible—there is also a purpose for Isaac to fulfill the promise that God made to Abraham—that Abraham would be the father of many nations. It is the same with you and me. Our Promised Seed of Purpose has been impregnated with purpose as well. Our Promised Seed of Purpose will produce after its own kind. Purpose will beget Purpose for the glory of God the Father.

God has given all of us dreams, visions, desires, and goals. He planted that Seed in your spirit and it is His will that you give birth to that Seed because it is needed in the Earth. Do not be deterred by any limitations you might perceive. Sarah gave birth at 89, Elizabeth gave birth at 87, Hannah was approximately 70, and Mary was about 14. Time has no effect on divine destiny. God is always on time.

You may be 40+, 50+, 60+, 70+, or 80+, but it is never too late to give birth to the Promised Seed of Purpose God has placed in your spirit. If you want to start that business, PUSH! If you want to start a ministry, PUSH! If you want to record your CD, PUSH! If you want to write your book, PUSH! God has equipped you with PURPOSE, His power and His strength. So, get ready to PUSH!

REFERENCES

[1] Retrieved from https://urbanministries.com/how-many-different-parts-are-in-your-body/

[2] https://helloclue.com/articles/cycle-a-z/what-is-sperm-what-are-human-eggs

[3] Ibid

[4] https://medlineplus.gov/ency/article/002220.htm

[5] Retrieved from https://www.bbc.com/news/health-32284075

[6] Retrieved from https://www.mayoclinic.org/diseases-conditions/pregnancy-loss-miscarriage/symptoms-causes/syc-20354298

[7] Retrieved from https://themindsjournal.com/intimacy-is-not-just-physical/

[8] Bruce Allen: Promise of the Third Day – Your Day of Destiny Has Arrived"

[9] J. O. Sanders, Enjoying Intimacy with God, p. 20

[10] Allen, B. (2007) Promise of the Third Day – Your Day of Destiny Has Arrived, Destiny Image Publshers, Inc. Shippenberg, PA

[11] AmericanPregnancy.org

[12] Retrieved from: https://www.mayoclinic.org/healthy-lifestyle/pregnancy-Week-by-Week/in-depth/high-risk-pregnancy/art-20047012 on November 27, 2018

[13] Bonnie Gray: Retrieved from http://thebonniegray.com/2012/01/why-you-cant-turn-back-when-youre-pregnant-with-a-promise/

[14] Ibid

[15] John Bloom, https://www.desiringgod.org/articles/why-gods-will-isnt-always-clear

[16] Sunday Adelaja: Retrieved from https://www.goodreads.com/quotes/tag/god-s-timing

[17] Retrieved from https://www.webmd.com/baby/pregnancy-amniocentesis#2-6

[18] Retrieved from https://www.thebump.com/pregnancy-week-by-week/20-weeks-pregnant

[19] Retrieved from https://www.webmd.com/baby/guide/your-pregnancy-week-by-week-weeks-21-25#1-

[20] "The Doctrine of Glory" by Paul Tripps https://www.paultripp.com/articles/posts/the-doctrine-of-glory-article

[21] James Goodlatte: "A Mother's Emotions Affect Her Unborn Child - Retrieved from https://getfitforbirth.com/a-mothers-emotions-affect-her-unborn-child/

[22] Retrieved from WebMD: https://www.webmd.com/baby/guide/third-trimester

[23] Health Direct: How Your Baby's Immune System Develops. Retrieved from https://www.pregnancybirthbaby.org.au/how-your-babys-immune-system-develops

[24] Taken from a T.D. Jakes sermon

Made in the USA
Middletown, DE
16 November 2022

15145966R00077